Enjoy your garden

FLOWERS IN COLOR

Edited by

FRANCIS B. STARK & CONRAD B. LINK

DOUBLEDAY & COMPANY, INC.

Horticultural Consultants: Francis C. Stark, Professor and Chairman, Department of Horticulture, University of Maryland; Conrad B. Link, Professor of Horticulture, University of Maryland

NOTE: The horticultural consultants have checked botanical terms against Bailey, *Standard Cyclopedia of Horticulture,* and other sources, but have used as the final authority Bailey and Bailey, *Hortus Second.* Some botanical varieties named by the authors have been retained even if they appear in none of our sources.

The original edition of this book was written in Italian, primarily for Italian gardeners. We have endeavored to preserve some of the rhetorical flavor of the Italian authors, while adapting the cultural and hardiness recommendations to the United States.

Picture Credits

Bevilacqua: cop.; Archivio I.G.D.A.: 10, 11, 12, 73, 120, 121, 178, 181, 193, 202; M. Bavestrelli: 21, 49, 74, 84, 85, 102, 114, 115, 136, 156, 199, 200; C. Bevilacqua: 4, 5, 15, 16, 26, 29, 30, 31, 33, 37, 38, 39, 42, 44, 52, 53, 54, 66, 67, 69, 70, 75, 76, 80, 94, 97, 98, 99, 107, 109, 118, 119, 128, 130, 135, 140, 141, 142, 143, 146, 147, 149, 150, 151, 153, 155, 158, 160, 161, 162, 163, 165, 166, 174, 175, 177, 179, 183, 185, 188, 211; Bravo: 137, 138, 144, 145; E.P.S.: 19, 65, 72, 77, 81, 111, 148, 168, 189, 194, 207; Etrusko: 2, 3, 7, 8, 13, 27, 28, 35, 40, 41, 43, 56, 60, 61, 91, 92, 96, 100, 112, 122, 134, 180, 198; Ingegnoli: 71, 167, 171, 173; P. Martini: 9, 45, 78, 93, 152, 172, 196, 201, 204, 206, 210; G. Mazza: 36, 63, 95, 117; M. Pedone: 1, 14, 57, 68, 89, 90, 110, 123, 132, 133, 157, 176, 184, 208, 209; P 2: 6, 17, 18, 20, 22, 23, 24, 25, 32, 34, 46, 47, 48, 50, 51, 55, 58, 59, 62, 64, 79, 82, 83, 86, 87, 88, 101, 103, 104, 105, 106, 108, 113, 116, 124, 125, 126, 127, 129, 131, 139, 154, 159, 164, 169, 170, 182, 186, 187, 190, 191, 192, 195, 197, 203, 205, 212, 213.

ISBN: 0-385-02933-0
Published under arrangement with
Ottenheimer Publishers, Inc.
Baltimore, Maryland
Manufactured in Italy by I.G.D.A.

Table of Contents

Introduction

From the largest of the public or private gardens to the most modest handkerchief-sized plot of earth covered with simple flowers, gardens have preserved an undeniable artistic and recreational value from legendary times to the present day.

Sometimes gardens are linked to the house in which we live; sometimes they are gardens for everyone, often placed in a large park where children play and, as a foreshadowing of their own future, meet older people reflecting on their past and remaking lost dreams.

As the earth makes its annual turn around the sun, the flowers give evidence of the passing of time. We have the flowers, varicolored, arranged in beds, in masses, and in the wild. They may be chaste white or flame-colored, sky-blue or mournful violet, set against a common, cool background of green leaves and a green lawn.

Within the "garden flowers" we include here the simpler herbaceous plants, those lacking a woody trunk and woody stems. In these pages, you will not find roses or the hydrangeas, but rather the bashful forget-me-not, the rustic cockscomb, fragrant hyacinths, and showy poppies, all having in common a short life, often only a year or two. During the constant change of seasons, spurred by the sun and guided by man, these many plants in association with each other beautify the earth and man's surroundings.

The sun makes their colors brilliant; man plans their arrangement and plants them, controls the timing of bloom, hybridizes and improves the species, and gathers seeds for the future, to make other gardens throughout the world.

This is a garden! A painting, a mobile, delicate, unstable fresco, whose colors and brush strokes are petals and leaves that come from an infinite palette and renew themselves from time to time in a scene that is changing and fixed simultaneously, to cheer the hearts and eyes of nameless admirers often required to look at them from the outside, beyond a fence marking the boundary with the public street.

The eyes admire the color and the form of flowers that may not be picked, while the mind tries to remember the foreign or Latin names heard or read, often without being able to associate them with one or another flower. And each would like to respond to the unsatisfied curiosity: a name, the name of a flower once known and now forgotten, one of the thousands and thousands of names of flowers among all those that ornament the gardens of the whole world.

A brief guide for the curious, this book is written to provide information to anyone wanting to know a little more about flowers: their names and cultural requirements, their origins and history, their variability and adaptation. Thus, from one page to another, a garden takes on life, simple and easy to grow, rich in colors, elegance, and fragrance, to compensate for all our work and effort. On a few square yards of earth we can grow both native and exotic plants, and assembled in a pleasing design, the resulting display rewards us.

Garden flowers

Authoritative sources report that the most ancient writings about garden flowers date back to more than 4,000 years ago. It is known that the Chinese, about 2,500 years before the beginning of the Christian era, were cultivating chrysanthemums. It is also known that the Egyptians, besides the lotus of the Nile and papyrus, grew myrtle and pomegranates. The Persians and the Babylonians were well acquainted with the culture of roses and violets. Finally, Pliny the Younger wrote about the culture of lilies and narcissus, of cyclamens and cornflowers.

The Middle Ages, though fostering the decline of civilization, kept alive the art and the interest in gardening, and whenever people returned from voyages to distant lands they always brought back new information on exotic flowers. And, coming back from long travels, every explorer took to Europe the seeds and bulbs of new plants, so that soon the gardens of France, Italy, Spain, and England were ornamented with rare, precious plants from the tropics.

It was thus that our floricultural inheritance slowly grew rich, and beside the native European flowers, such as the cornflowers and violets, already improved beyond their wild state, appeared geraniums from South Africa, hyacinths from the Orient, petunias from America, and poppies from Asia.

Thus the number of garden flowers—those to which we will refer here, not including woody plants or shrubs—increased rapidly and continues to increase. The number of species and cultivated varieties (more correctly called "cultivars") number in the tens of thousands.

The choice available is practically unlimited, and we can cater to our varying tastes and plans, but the choice is limited by climatic adaptation of the species. Everyone knows that there are plants for cold climates, plants for temperate climates, and plants for tropical climates. Each type, in order to live, or at least in order to blossom—which is what we ask of garden flowers—needs a suitable temperature, a certain degree of moisture both in the soil and in the air, and an appropriate length of daylight.

It is also known, however, that with correct cultural practice and protection it is possible to have tropical plants in gardens located in regions of cool-temperate climates, even though they can live outside, unprotected, for only a short season.

Even a modest garden must have available a small protective structure to maintain suitable temperatures for growing seedlings, unless one wants to grow only the simpler plants that are adapted to germinate and continue all their life cycle outdoors. These plants are not lacking, especially among the annual kinds; remember the petunias, poppies, daisies, pansies, and a thousand others!

Soil

In addition to ecological and climatic influences, two other important fundamentals for good results in growing garden flowers are the soil and water.

Plants are living organisms, often very delicate, not always economical, and each species performs best in a particular type of soil: sometimes a heavier soil, sometimes lighter and sandier. Sometimes the soil should be of mineral origin, whereas some species grow best in organic soils, such as peats or mucks. One should remember that all the characteristics of the soil determine its water-holding capacity, so that moisture requirements are related to the types of soil in the garden.

Basic to the success of any garden is the soil. Unfortunately, most home owners do not buy a house for the soil surrounding it, and the garden must start with the soil as it is. Some soil problems are the result of the house-construction process, such as the use of heavy equipment and trucks on the lot during rainy periods. Spreading of excavated earth over the native soil at final grading is usually deleterious.

The ideal garden soil is a sandy loam, loam, or silt loam, having 1% or more organic matter and a pH of 6.0 to 6.5.

Some ericaceous plants, such as azaleas, prefer a soil pH of 5.0, although most plants thrive best at pH 6.0 to 6.5. Soils low in pH can be limed for correction, but a pH test should be performed to determine the amount of lime needed. pH tests are performed by many agencies; the gardener is advised to check with his county Extension agent on where this service can be rendered.

Soils having pH 7.0 or higher (common in western U.S.) can be corrected by the addition of sulfur, but the usual thing is to grow those plants that do well on high-calcium soils.

Soils low in organic matter can be improved by the addition of organic materials, but the basic texture of the soil cannot be materially changed except at great expense. Soils are composed of particles of sand, silt and clay. Particle size is as follows:

Sand—0.05 to 2.00 mm.
Silt—0.002 to 0.05 mm.
Clay—smaller than 0.002 mm.

It is the mix of these particles that determines soil texture. A loam will contain about 20–25% sand, 20–50% silt, and 8–28% clay. A sandy loam contains more sand and less silt and clay. A silt loam contains more silt and less sand than a loam. Sandy soils are considered "light" and easiest to manage, while those with higher percentages of clay are called "heavy" and are more difficult to manage. The heaviest soils, the clays and the clay loams, present special problems to the gardener, but can be improved in time by incorporation of sand and organic materials. Sandy soils can best be improved by using practices designed to increase the organic matter content.

Organic materials most commonly used to enhance the soil texture and to increase water-holding capacity are compost, leaves, wood chips and peat moss.

A composted soil is essentially a mixture, made in advance, by building a pile of alternate layers of soil and organic materials. This organic matter may be leaves, garden refuse, straw, animal manures, or any inexpensive organic material. Six to eight months after such a pile has been constructed, it is ready to use. Cut the pile down in such a manner that the soil and organic matter are mixed. To speed up the process of rotting, the pile may be cut down and rebuilt before use. Fertilizers such as superphosphate and some nitrogen forms may be included as the pile is built.

Leaves, wood chips, and peat moss are used as a mulch and should be applied thickly enough to inhibit weed growth. When the garden is reworked the following spring for the new crop of annuals, these materials are turned under and a new mulch applied after planting. After a few years, this practice will materially improve most soils.

Watering the garden

The indispensability of water for the survival of plants needs little explanation; one need only realize that most vegetative tissues are 85 to 95% water. Water should therefore never be lacking in order to avoid wilting, and should wilting be prolonged and reach the physiological limit for permanent wilting, death of the plant will result.

Annual plants with succulent leaves, such as cinerarias and calceolarias, are especially subject to desiccation, while those with small leaves and stiff stems, such as carnations, are much more tolerant. Those plants with tubers, rhizomes, or bulbs are most tolerant to drought, since their underground stems serve as a reserve for water and minerals.

The amount of water needed by various flowering species is extremely variable. Some plants are hygrophilic (requiring a large amount of water), mesophilic (having a moderate water requirement), or xerophilic (that is, thriving under very dry conditions), with every intermediate stage.

The necessary amount of water varies also with the climatic, regional, and seasonal conditions, and depends also upon the soil texture and organic matter content, as well as upon the nature of the subsoil.

Generally, in home gardens, the amount of water needed is rather modest and an inch of rainfall or irrigation every 5 to 7 days should be adequate. The soil should be kept loose and permeable with timely weeding and tilling to prevent the formation of surface crusting.

Hand weeding is best for the maintenance of the water balance of cultivated ground, since the invading plants often absorb more water than the flowering plants. All weeds are harmful to the garden, and the invading species vary.

Drought is especially dangerous when seedlings are very small and therefore tender and delicate. Overwatering is equally dangerous.

To avoid extreme transpiration and to inhibit weed growth, a mulch of leaves, peat moss, tanbark, straw, or plastic is desirable.

Watering may be done at any time, but mid-afternoon watering should be discouraged in areas of high light intensity. Water droplets on the leaves after the irrigation is complete may act like small magnifying glasses and concentrate the sun's rays, resulting in localized leaf burn.

Fertilizing the garden

Referring earlier to the various types of soil, we mentioned organic matter and pH, both of extreme importance to the cultivation of plants. But soils contain numerous chemical elements, present in greater or lesser quantities, including calcium, nitrogen, potassium, phosphorus, manganese, iron, sulfur, magnesium, boron, copper, zinc, molybdenum, bromine, tungsten, silicon, and still others. Some are indispensable to plant growth, whereas others, such as the last three named, are unnecessary to plants. These compounds are also present in organic residues.

Nitrogen, phosphorus, and potassium are the three nutrient elements that are most commonly lacking in soil and that are added as fertilizers. Such materials may be added in a dry form as the soil is prepared or in a liquid form after the plant has been planted. The liquid types are water soluble and may be applied in very dilute concentrations every time the plant is watered or in a more concentrated form less frequently. The inorganic fertilizers, in either the dry or liquid form, may supply only one element or, in certain cases, two elements. Commercial mixtures generally supply the three nutrient elements named and often include one or more of the so-called minor elements such as iron, boron, or manganese which, in very minute quantities, are necessary for plant growth.

The inorganic fertilizers are the least expensive to use, when based on the amount of nutrients they supply. Organic fertilizers are not available to the plant until they have been decomposed.

Inorganic fertilizer sources are those manufactured especially or that are by-products of certain manufacturing processes. These include ammonium sulfate, calcium sulfate, sodium nitrate, ammonium nitrate, and urea that supply nitrogen; superphosphate which supplies phosphorus; and potassium chloride or potassium sulfate that supply potassium.

The inorganic fertilizers have their origin primarily from certain animals, as a by-product. Organic nitrogen sources include horn and hoof shavings, dried blood, and fish meal; phosphorus may be supplied from bonemeal; and wood ashes are an organic source of potassium. Organic fertilizers may vary slightly from time to time in the exact amount of fertilizer element they supply, and may actually contribute traces of some other elements when decomposing. This is influenced by the treatment followed in processing for fertilizer use.

Lime is not considered to be a fertilizer; rather its greatest effect is to make the soil less acid and to help improve soil structure. Calcium does become available to the plant from the lime incorporated in the soil.

Animal manures are not commonly available and are variable as to their fertility value which is influenced by the kind of animal, its diet, the amount of bedding material included, and the care of the manure before application to the soil. The greatest value of manure is not as a fertilizer, but rather as a source of organic matter which has a beneficial influence on improving soil structure.

For the home gardener, it will be most convenient to use commercially-prepared fertilizers, which are usually mixtures of materials that supply nitrogen, phosphorus, and potassium and are referred to as a "complete fertilizer." Such kinds are available both in a dry form to be mixed into the soil in advance of planting or as a top dressing, or are made of water soluble materials that can be dissolved in water and applied to the soil as a liquid.

A newer fertilizer type is the slow-release or slow-acting kind that may be mixed into the soil and remains effective for many months. One form is a soluble material "encapsulated" into a plastic-like material which, when in contact with the soil moisture, gradually releases the fertilizer to the soil solution, and is then available to the plant.

Seeding

Almost every plant that bears flowers can be reproduced by seed, because this is the natural process for its reproduction. In gardening practice, we frequently find it easier to propagate some flowering plants vegetatively, that is by cuttings, grafting, or layering, and these methods are discussed later.

Propagation by seed is the best way to grow annual flowers. Annuals are the easiest of all plants to grow, and they require no care or space after flowering since they die after completing their life cycle. To this group, with some exceptions, belong the morning glories, marigolds, pansies, petunias, poppies, zinnias, and many other beautiful flowers.

Biennial plants—those that complete their life cycle in two years—are also reproduced by seed. In certain cases they live longer than two years and are sometimes propagated by cuttings.

Perennials are hardier plants that usually live for several years and can be reproduced by seed, but they often are increased by cuttings, especially in cases in which flowers do not bear seeds to maturation, such as the fuchsias; or where they are sterile or do not produce seed, as in the case of double flowers.

Some seeds are sown in the area where they are to grow. Plants that do not transplant easily are handled in this way, sown in place. Among our ornamental plants, this is necessary for only a few kinds of annuals. Most seed is sown in a medium that is loose, porous, well aerated and yet will hold water. Such a medium can be prepared by mixing soil with organic matter and perhaps some inert material. In outdoor beds this may be accomplished by selecting a suitable spot with well-drained soil. Mixtures of materials include peat and perlite, or peat and vermiculite; other mixtures might include soil, sand, or similar inert substances.

Seed may be sown in beds out of doors or in the home at a window, in a greenhouse, or in protective frames such as a cold frame or hot bed. Seed should be scattered over the the seed bed uniformly and then be lightly covered. Tiny seeds such as those of begonia, calceolaria, petunia, or azalea are not covered, but are merely pressed into the soil. For seed of these kinds, covering the soil with a thin layer of finely-screened sphagnum makes a good material for the seed.

When the seed has germinated, thin out the weak seedlings and those that are crowded to allow those remaining to have greater space for development. When the seedlings have developed their first true leaf they are ready for transplanting. Transplant them to seed beds, spacing them to allow for development and then later transplant them again to where they are to grow. Or they may be transplanted to pots, flats, or other containers. Rapidly-growing kinds are often transplanted from the seed bed to the place where they are to grow to full development.

Transplanting

When sowing is completed, germination will take place within a few days for annuals, or may require several weeks with certain perennials and woody plants. The new plants, just after emerging from the soil, are extremely delicate, and sudden, extreme changes in temperature must be avoided, as should exposure to full sun or excessive water.

As soon as the plants begin to grow, they show the morphological characteristics of the species to which they belong and may be distinguished from any other plants that may surround them which have been derived from seeds already present in the sowing medium or perhaps from seeds mixed with the seed sown.

Weeds must be removed with care, and this is most easily done at the time of thinning or transplanting.

Thinning is required to give space to seedlings that spring up too closely to each other. This may be accomplished by transplanting the seedlings into separate pots. Sometimes it is convenient to transplant seedlings to their permanent site, outdoors.

Transplanting must be done with some care to avoid bruising or breaking the young plants.

To remove a plant from a pot, it is best to overturn it, keeping the stem between the fingers and tapping lightly on the sides of the pot in order to remove the ball of soil.

Thinning is best done during the cooler hours of the day. Afterwards, the soil should be firmed gently around the plants and they should be sprinkled lightly. Thinned or transplanted seedlings should be protected from direct sunlight for two days.

Vegetative propagation

Since plants produced from seed may not come true-to-type or may require too long a period of time before coming into flower or developing mature characteristics, a vegetative method is often selected. Plants vary in the part of the plant that may be used for propagation; depending on the kind of plant, it may be the stem, the leaves, or the roots. In some plants vegetative methods merely use the parts of the plant that naturally account for the increase, such as the bulbs, tubers, rhizomes, stolons, or off-shoot runners. Propagation may also be achieved by dividing of the plant which involves its separation into smaller parts by layering, or by grafting or budding.

Tubers, bulbs, rhizomes, and runners are all essentially stems that are somewhat modified and that have the ability to produce new roots when they are separated from the mother plant. When they are removed, they already have the beginnings of new roots and are ready for replanting.

Layering is a form of propagation where a branch is bent down to the soil and covered, leaving the tip exposed. Often a wound is made in the stem portion that is covered. After roots develop, the branch is cut at the end nearest the parent and the new plant is replanted. Air layering is a method often used on foliage plants that have become too tall. A wound is made in the stem, a bit of wood is placed in the cut to hold it open, and the wound is dusted with a root-promoting hormone. The entire area is covered with moist sphagnum moss and wrapped with plastic or aluminum foil. The moss must be kept moist. After roots have developed into the moss, the stem is severed below this area and the tip now with developing roots is potted as a new plant. Air layering may be used on a few woody plants outdoors.

Cuttings are perhaps the most common method of vegetative propagation. Cuttings are made from strong, healthy stems. The tip is used, generally with 3 to 4 nodes, varying with the kind of plant, and often similar sections of the lower portions of the stem can be selected as well. The season of propagation varies with the plant. Soft immature growth is not satisfactory; rather it should be fully developed, although the growth may not need to be fully mature. Such growth is referred to as a soft-wood cutting or as a greenwood or herbaceous cutting. Other cuttings may be semi-woody or fully developed and woody. Cuttings are propagated in sand, peat, perlite, or vermiculite or perhaps some other inert, pest-free material. Some gardeners will make a mixture of these kinds. Loose porous soil is also used especially when propagating outdoors.

In the greenhouse, propagation is done in a shaded location, either by shading the plants or the glass above. The humidity should be high.

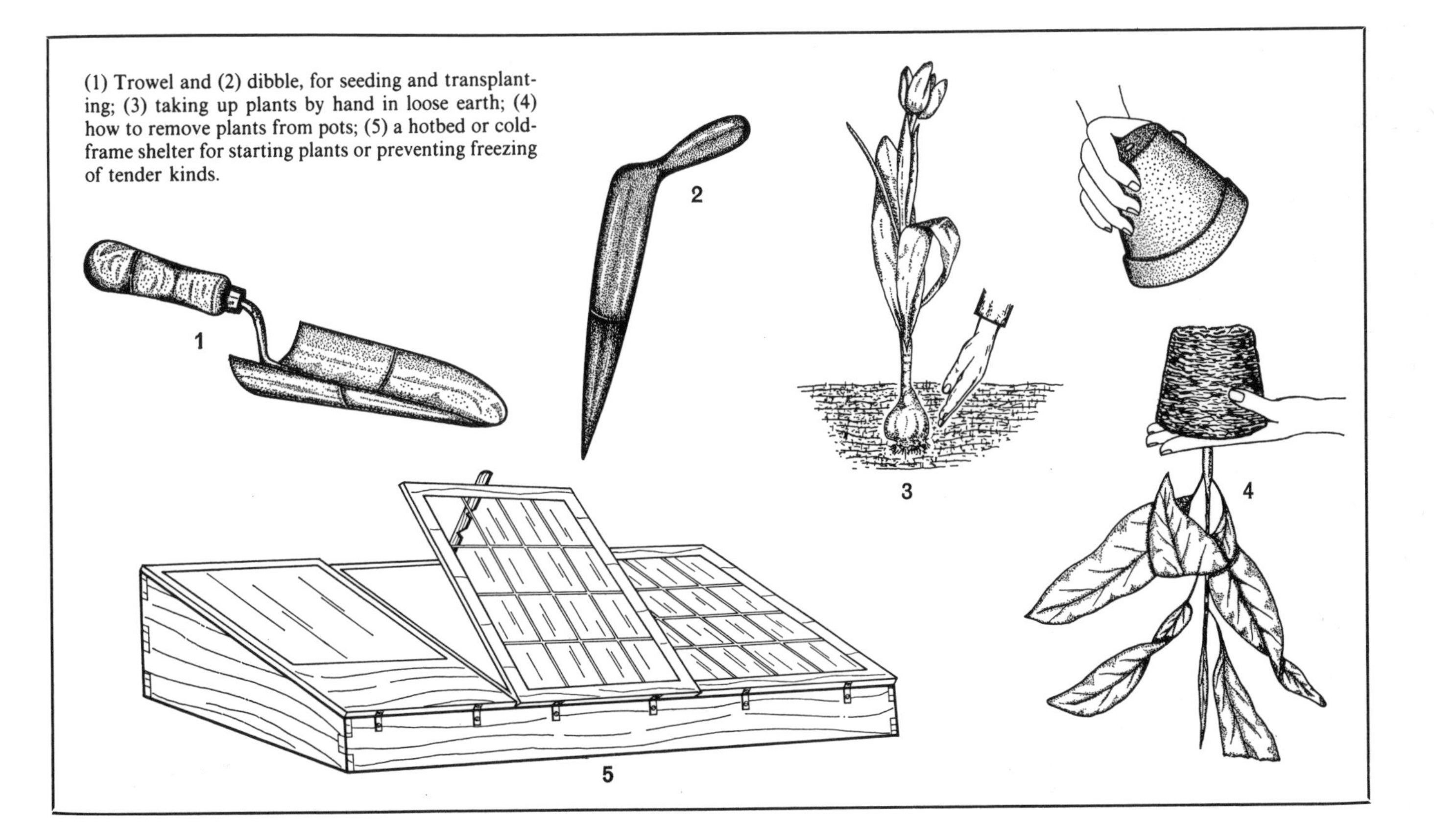

(1) Trowel and (2) dibble, for seeding and transplanting; (3) taking up plants by hand in loose earth; (4) how to remove plants from pots; (5) a hotbed or coldframe shelter for starting plants or preventing freezing of tender kinds.

During the fall, winter, and spring months, the rooting of many cuttings is hastened if the medium is several degrees warmer than the air temperature. Heating pipes located below the propagation bench or the use of an electric heating cable are ways in which this can be accomplished.

Root-promoting chemicals speed up the time of rooting and ensure that a higher percentage of cuttings will root. Commercial preparations of these are available in either a dry or liquid form. The dry form is a powder, and the stem end is dipped into it before it is placed in the propagation medium. The liquid kinds are either ready to use or need to be diluted with water. In either case, the stem end is dipped into or soaked in the solution before being put into the medium. These preparations are available in small-sized packages for the home gardener. They contain chemicals such as indoleacetic acid, indole-butyric acid, or salts of these acids with other related chemicals.

The leaves from certain types of plants may be used for propagation. Mature leaves are removed from a plant such as *Saintpaulia* and inserted into a propagating medium in the same manner as a stem cutting. A new plant will develop at the base and when it is large enough to handle conveniently, it is potted as a new plant. Leaves of peperomia may be handled in the same way. Leaves of certain begonias, especially *Begonia Rex,* are laid on a moist propagation medium and new plants will develop at the base as well as at any wound that is made in the large leaf veins. Leaves of the *Sansevieria* may be cut into sections 2 to 3 inches long and treated in the same way.

Division is a simple method of propagation and is used for those plants that form a cluster of many stems. The plant is removed from the pot, and the stems or crowns cut apart into smaller pieces. Usually this is done when the plant is in its least active period of growth. The practice is the same as that used for perennial plants outdoors.

Grafting and the related technique of budding are seldom used for garden plants. An appropriate understock is selected and a scion of the desired plant is attached or the bud inserted. The methods of taking care of the grafted or budded plants and the season of the year in which it is done vary with the kind of plant. Fruit trees, some azaleas, roses and lilacs are familiar plants that are grafted. Cactus are sometimes grafted, to produce odd-shaped plants; an example is the practice of grafting the Christmas Cactus, *Schlumbergera* or *Zygocactus,* onto *Pereskia* to form a tree-like plant.

Selection and hybridization

All plants that reproduce by seed have, in their genetic complexity, the characteristics already present in their parent plants: those that in fertilization produced the seed. It is obvious that all plants emerging from seed which has been produced and self-fertilized by a single plant—and these self-pollinated types are numerous—will be identical in their qualitative characteristics: form of the leaves and general structure and flower color, for example.

In a population of flowering plants we may often notice, however, variability among offspring into those of greater or lesser height and those with more or fewer flowers, for example. These are considered to be quantitative characteristics.

Observing this variability among several individual plants of the same cultivar, gardeners make a primary selection by collecting seed only from the most vigorous and healthy plants. This results in the isolation of special strains, or breeds, of a cultivar that will perpetuate a particular characteristic (for example, early flowering or color intensity) even though the basic qualitative characters remain unchanged.

We recall that plants propagated vegetatively will be identical to the parent plant since, without sexual union, genetic variability that can occur with natural hybridization is prevented. Cross-fertilization of one plant with another results in an equal mix of genes from the female and the male parents in the seed. This cross-fertilization is called hybridization, and is employed by plant breeders to develop new cultivars or horticultural varieties. Hybridization may result naturally from cross-pollination effected by wind or by insects, or it may be performed by man to obtain controlled crosses so that the male as well as the female parent is known. Artificial hybridization consists of taking pollen from the anthers of one flower and putting it on the stigma of a flower on another related plant. By this technique, the plant breeder induces fertilization and employs his knowledge of Mendelian and cytoplasmic inheritance to induce variation within succeeding generations.

Usually the plants used as parents belong to the same botanical species or at least to the same genus. Crosses between plants of two different genera are rarely successful, and in some cases crosses between two species of the same genus are difficult. For example, the pollen of a zinnia flower (genus *Zinnia*) will fertilize flowers of the same species of zinnia, and an attempt to fertilize flowers of other species of zinnias has a high probability of success. But zinnia pollen will not fertilize the flowers of some other plants similar in appearance, such as asters (genus *Aster*) or China asters (genus *Callistephus*), because the genetic makeup of these distinct genera is very different.

Artificial hybridization can give surprising, often unexpected results since it is not always possible to know the genetic background of the parent plants used for pollination. This is the reason why horticulturists have obtained—often accidentally—hybrids with flowers quite exceptional in color, in shape, or in size. The range of offerings among the dahlias and chrysanthemums emphasizes the possibilities.

One should be aware, however, that not all pollination results in the production of fertile seed, and if not fertile, the seeds will not germinate. In other cases, the plants resulting from hybridization may be less beautiful and less colorful, with smaller flowers than those of either parent. Occasionally, these "reversions" are successful, producing strains of dwarf plants or those with tiny flowers (*parviflora* varieties) of particular value.

Artificial hybridization is an operation that can be performed rather easily, especially when the plants have large flowers, and even more particularly when they have a large ovary, a conspicuous stigma, and very distinct anthers. In selecting which of two plants to be hybridized shall be the female parent, it is generally better to utilize the more vigorous plant or the one with larger flowers for this purpose.

One must remove the anthers from the flowers that will be the female parent before pollen is shed, to prevent self-pollination. The flowers thus emasculated are then enclosed in a cloth or paper bag to prevent insect or wind pollination. Frequently the stigma is receptive to pollen before the pollen in the same flower is shed, permitting emasculation and cross-pollination to be done at the same time. In other species, it is necessary to delay pollination for from 12 to 24 hours. Pollen is placed on the stigma by direct contact with an anther or by a small brush which has lightly swept a mature anther of the flower selected to be the male parent. For sticky pollen and that gathered in small masses, slender tweezers or wooden splinters are used.

Once pollination is completed, the flower is again protected by the bag to prevent outside pollination. If the operation has been successful, the ovary will enlarge slowly, and the bag should be removed. The flower should be tagged to identify its parentage when the cross is made.

The seeds are collected when mature and should be stored in paper envelopes on which the parentage of the seed is indicated. The parentage is indicated by writing the name of the female first, followed by an "X" (meaning "cross-pollinated") and then the name of the male parent.

By international convention, the varieties of plants not naturally found in the wild but developed by hybridization and/or selection are called cultivars—that is, culvated varieties.

Garden pests

There are several major groups of garden pests, including insects, diseases, physiological disorders, and other animal pests and weeds. The latter are not discussed in this section.

Plants which suffer from physiological problems often appear as if they had been affected by an insect or a disease. Leaf damage or irregularities may be caused by a mineral deficiency or excess, especially of the three major elements most commonly lacking from soils (nitrogen, phosphorus and potassium) and on occasion, other elements such as magnesium or boron. A lack of each element produces a distinctive reaction in the plant, and yet the deficiency is difficult to diagnose since some diseases may show similar symptoms. Toxic substances in the atmosphere may cause marginal injury to leaves or interfere with normal leaf development.

Improper conditions in the environment such as excess or insufficient sun for a particular species may cause unnatural growth, such as foliage that is excessively large or small or an unnatural leaf color for that plant. Constant excess or lack of water in the soil will influence plant growth and eventually the size, and perhaps flower formation as well. Soil problems are corrected by the proper fertilizer applications while excess applications can sometimes be leached from the soil by frequent heavy watering provided the soil has good drainage.

Oedemia, the development of swellings or outgrowths on the lower side of the leaf of certain plants, is associated with an excessive supply of water in the soil and high humidity. It is peculiarly a greenhouse problem and uncommon in the garden.

The more typical diseases include the virus diseases and those caused by bacteria or by fungi.

Virus diseases are caused by a submicroscopic organism that spreads rapidly through the infected plant. It is spread by contact from an affected plant to a healthy one. It is found in the vascular system and generally there is no control. Some virus diseases develop so rapidly that the plant is dwarfed, and shows characteristic leaf patterns of green and yellow. A few virus diseases seem to do little damage and may be present without injury to the plant. This is true for some variegated plants, where the variegation is actually caused by a virus. Most virus diseases are rather specific for a given plant while others may infect many kinds. There are no effective controls for virus other than to use care in selecting propagating material and to rogue out infected plants.

Bacterial diseases develop when bacteria enter the plant through a wound. Many rot and decay diseases are caused by bacteria, as well as certain leaf spots, leaf blights, and galls.

Fungi cause other types of injury; again, they may appear as a leaf spot, a leaf blight, as cankers on a stem, as mildew, or as rust on a leaf or stem. Diseases that cause the plant to wilt are also caused by a fungus.

Damping off, the dying of seedlings and young plants by rotting at the soil line or just below, may be caused by several disease organisms. Soil sterilization and seed or soil treatment with a fungicide are effective controls, actually precautions for the prevention of this problem.

To control diseases in a garden, first be certain that the soil and environment are correct for the plant, then remove infected parts if possible, and use a recommended fungicide, following directions on the label. Disease controls are constantly changing, but currently recommended fungicides include ferbam, captan, as well as zinc, sulfur, and copper-containing materials.

Insect pests include the aphids, thrips, scale insects, leaf-chewing kinds, and spider mites. White fly may be a problem during periods of low rainfall. Insects may attack many kinds of plants in contrast to certain diseases that infect only one species or closely-related species.

Aphids typically are found on rapidly-growing tips of plants and injure the plant by sucking the juices. Thrips are very tiny and feed on the underside of the leaf, sucking the juices and causing a silvery appearance on the surface. Scale insects are sucking insects that attach themselves to stems and leaves and are covered with a waxy or shell-like covering which makes them more difficult to control. Mealy bugs are soft white insects, "mealy" in appearance, found in the axils of the leaves and at the tip, and cause damage by sucking the plant sap. Control is difficult because of this waxy covering. Cyclamen mites attack the growing shoots of the African violet, cyclamen, begonia, gloxinia and other gesneriads, causing the new growth to be stunted or deformed, and often preventing the plant from developing properly. White Fly is a small white insect from the tropics and can become difficult to control. The adults are moth-like, covered with a white waxy powder, and fly about when the plant is disturbed. This insect lays its eggs on the underside of the leaves of many greenhouse plants and may be transported outdoors with the plants. The immature stages are a pale greenish color, semi-transparent, and cause damage by sucking the plant juices. Lantana, cineraria, fuchsia, ageratum, tomatoes, poinsettias are favorites of this insect.

The control of insects involves using a spray or dust. The recommended materials are being altered so rapidly to conform to acceptable safety standards that commercial preparations should be selected for control. Many insects are most easily controlled when they are in their immature stages, and the plant should be thoroughly covered with the material, both on the top and the lower side of the leaf. It is a good practice to inspect all plants for pests before transplanting them and to spray them first. Sometimes a thorough washing of the foliage with warm soapy water will dislodge the pests, and this is followed by a clear water wash to remove the suds. Syringing of the plants with water under a spray-like force will dislodge many insects, and if done routinely this may provide control.

There is still another group of insect-related pests, not true insects, but for practical purposes often considered with them, that will cause damage. These include sowbugs or pillbugs, oval-shaped pests with many legs, that curl into a ball when disturbed. Millipedes also have many legs and are typically dark, shiny brown, and move rapidly. These two pests are common in areas where organic matter accumulates, as under a mulch or in a compost pile. Generally they are harmless to growing plants. They may sometimes attack germinating seed and seedlings. Slugs, slimy snails without a shell, and snails with a shell may be a nuisance because they feed not only on decaying matter but on seedlings or on soft succulent leaves and new growth. Control for these is by bait such as metaldehyde or beer.

Nematodes are still another soil pest that may attack the root and some forms attack the leaves. These are also called eel worms; they penetrate the tissue and in the case of roots may cause a swelling or an enlargement. Foliage nematodes effect damage by causing spots or sections of a leaf to turn brown, as on begonia or the chrysanthemum. For soil nematodes, soil sterilization is the best control; the planting of pest-free material is also advantageous. Foliar types are controlled by sprays.

Garden design and the lawn

The lawn is an essential part of the design of most gardens. It often is the greatest area of the garden and, when well kept, adds luster to the other plants, the flowers, shrubs, and trees: in short, the lawn is the green carpet.

In designing a garden, plan it in such a way that it will be easy to maintain. Avoid styles or designs with many small areas, isolated specimen plants and beds, or garden ornaments. To obtain a feeling of space, allow as much open unplanted space as possible.

Consider the use of the garden and develop the plan to allow for the activities it can provide. It may be an area for children to play, a sitting area with a picnic table and fireplace, an area for pets, a place for home sports, or for a small greenhouse. In your design, develop areas where you can grow your favorite plants, a rose garden, space for a flower hobby such as dahlias or gladioli, for annuals, perennials, a bed of strawberries, or a vegetable garden. Take advantage of existing features on your property: for example, if you have large trees and much shade, then develop a woodland garden with plants suitable for these conditions; a low area may suggest a natural-looking pool, or a slope may be the place for a rock garden. Consider the architectural features of the house and develop the garden to fit that style.

Lawns are made up primarily of grasses, generally a mixture of two or more kinds appropriate to the climatic conditions. In the northern part of the United States where there are cold winters and mild summers, the "cool" season grasses are used. These include Kentucky bluegrass *(Poa pratensis),* fine-leaf fescue *(Festuca rubra),* bent grass *(Agrostis tenius),* and creeping bent grass *(Agrostis palustris).* There are several strains or selections of each of these with slight variations in their characteristics and their adaptability. Often several are included in commercial grass-seed mixtures. These are all considered fine-textured grasses. For play areas or athletic fields, the course-textured grasses such as tall fescue *(Festuca elatior)* and perennial ryegrass *(Lolium perenne)* are used. They are tough and will withstand rough play.

Cool season grasses are seeded in the fall or early spring. After the area has been graded, thoroughly prepare the soil, rake carefully, and then sow the seed. The rate of seeding for lawn purposes is 2 to 3 pounds to 1000 square feet; this rate should be doubled for playgrounds and athletic fields.

It is recommended that soil tests be made to determine the need for lime and fertilizers. Lawn grasses will grow best in a slightly acid soil, pH 6.0 to 6.5. As the soil is being prepared for seeding, incorporate liberal quantities of thoroughly decomposed organic matter, such as manures or sawdust, especially on heavy-textured soils. Add the necessary fertilizer and the lime that may be required to correct the acidity.

Fertilizing an established lawn is generally done by using a complete fertilizer with a high amount of nitrogen and medium levels of phosphorus and potash, unless a soil test indicates otherwise. Such lawns are fertilized in early fall and again in early spring. More frequent fertilization is done where special attention is given to watering at other seasons.

Grasses that are better adapted to the warmer areas of the United States include Bermuda grass *(Cynodon dactylon)* and zoysia *(Zoysia matrella),* and, for the more southern areas, include, in addition, centipede grass *(Eremochloa ophiuroides),* St. Augustine grass *(Stenotaphrum secundatum),* and bahia grass *(Paspalum notatum).* Several of these southern grasses are propagated by cutting or tearing apart established sod into small pieces and sowing or planting as "sprigs." Plugs of sod may be planted in existing lawns to gradually replace the present grass or may be used to establish a new lawn. The soil is prepared as if for new seeding.

Redtop *(Agrostis alba)* and annual ryegrass *(Lolium multiflorum)* are often in lawn seed mixtures because they germinate and grow quickly. They are short lived but serve to give the permanent grasses a chance to become established. They are referred to as "nurse" grasses.

Lawns need to be fertilized regularly depending on the growth and climate. Mowing frequently gives a well-groomed apperance. Blue grass and fescue lawns should be mowed not shorter than 2 to 3 inches. Water should be applied liberally when the soils become dry to wet down to a depth of 4 to 6 inches. Avoid frequent sprinkling.

Sodding with a good quality sod gives an immediate lawn. To sod a lawn, the soil should be as carefully prepared and fertilized as if seed were to be sown. After the sod has been laid, it is rolled and then watered. In a few days it will become established.

Glossary

*1. **Achene**—a dry, hard, indehiscent, single-seeded fruit with a single carpel.
2. **Acaulescent**—stemless
3. **Acuminate**—tapering to a point.
4. **Adnate**—united, grown together.
5. **Adventitious**—originating at other than the usual place; *roots* originating from any structure other than a root; *buds* arising from a part of the plant other than terminal or node.
6. **Alternate** (leaves)—one leaf at each node but alternating in direction.
7. **Annual**—a plant with a one-year life cycle.
8. **Anther**—that part of the stamen containing the pollen.
9. **Apetalous**—lacking petals.
10. **Apical**—terminal or summit.
11. **Axil**—the angle between a leaf and stem.
*12. **Berry**—a simple, fleshy fruit developed from a single ovule (loosely, any pulpy or juicy fruit).
13. **Biennial**—a plant with a two-year life cycle.
14. **Blade**—the expanded part of a leaf or leaflet.
*15. **Blossom**—the flower of a seed plant.
16. **Bract**—a specialized, modified leaf; of leaf-like structure.
17. **Bud**—a compressed stem; an underdeveloped stem.
18. **Bulb**—underground storage and reproductive organ with fleshy leaves called bulb scales.
19. **Calyx**—the outermost of the floral parts, composed of sepals.
*20. **Campanulate**—bell-shaped.
21. **Capitate**—shaped like a head.
*22. **Capsule**—a dry, dehiscent, multi-seeded fruit of more than one carpel.
23. **Carpel**—a leaf-like structure bearing ovules along the margins; a simple pistil.
*24. **Cauline**—related to an obvious stem or axis.
25. **Comose**—having tufts of hair.
*26. **Cordate**—heart-shaped.
27. **Corm**—an enlarged, underground stem, serving as a storage organ for food reserves.
28. **Corolla**—an inner cycle of floral organs, comprising the petals.
29. **Corymb**—a flat-topped, indeterminate flower cluster, with pedicels originating along a central peduncle; outer flowers open first.
30. **Cotyledons**—the first (seed) leaves of the embryo.
31. **Crenate**—toothed with rounded teeth.
32. **Crispate**—curled.
33. **Culm**—the stem of a grass or sedge.
34. **Cultivar**—a variety developed from known hybridization or origin.
35. **Cuneate**—triangular, wedge-shaped.
36. **Cyme**—a determinate flower cluster in which the central flower opens first.
37. **Deciduous**—plants that drop their leaves at the end of each season.
38. **Dehiscent**—opening of an anther or a fruit, permitting escape of pollen or seeds.
39. **Dentate**—toothed along the margins, apex sharp.
40. **Dichotomous**—divided into pairs; forked branches roughly equal.
41. **Dicotyledonous**—having two cotyledons.

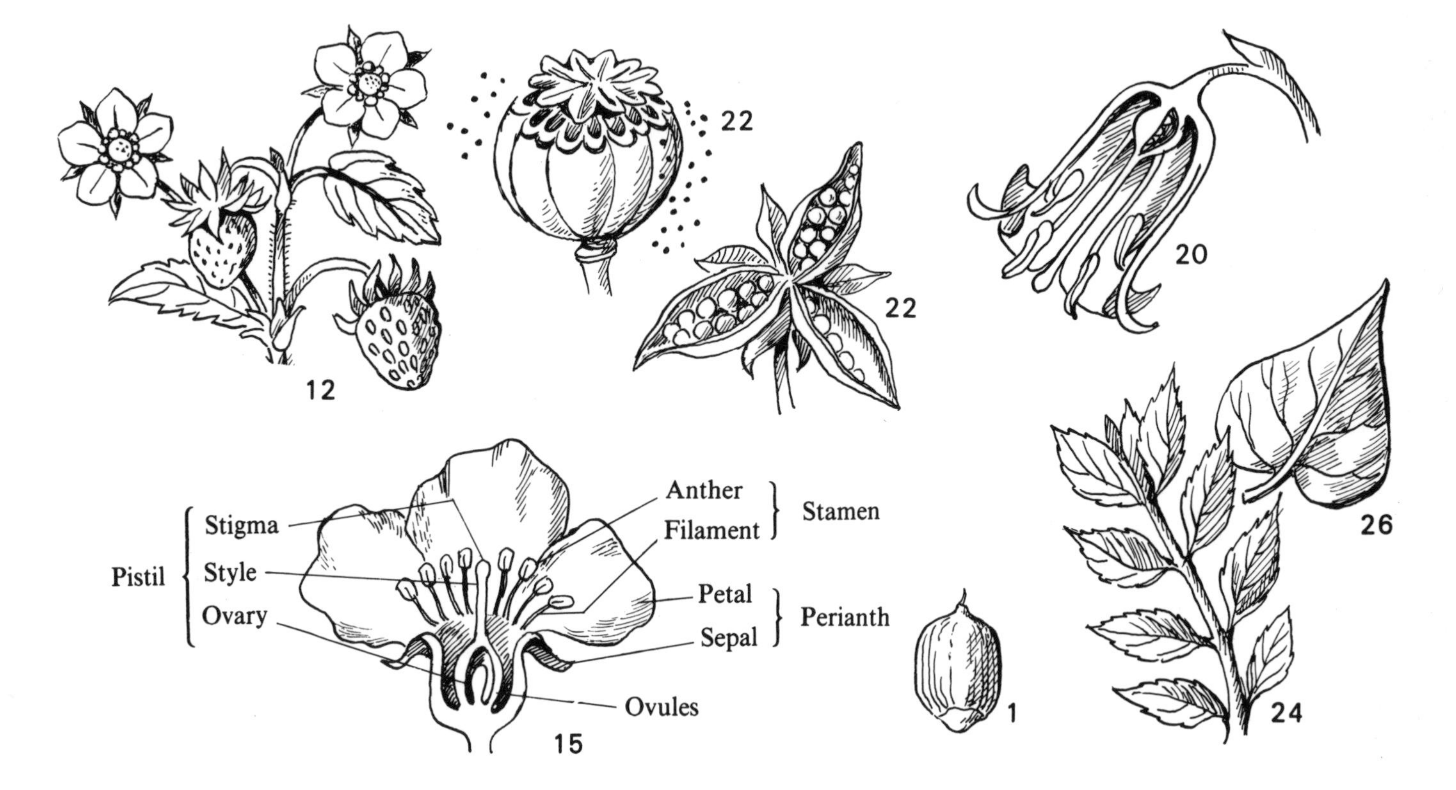

42. **Digitate** (leaves)—with leaflets arising from the apex of the petiole.
43. **Dioecious**—a species having male and female flowers on different, individual plants.
44. **Distichous**—in two vertical ranks, as the leaves of grasses.
*45. **Drupe**—a simple fleshy fruit, single carpel, with a hard endocarp containing the seed, e.g., the peach.
46. **Embryo**—a rudimentary plant.
47. **Entire**—without dentation or division.
48. **Epiphyte**—a plant that grows on another but is not parasitic.
49. **Fasciated**—an abnormally wide and flat stem.
50. **Filament**—the part of the stamen supporting the anther.
51. **Follicle**—a dry, dehiscent fruit with a single carpel, which dehisces along the ventral suture.
52. **Frond**—the leaf of a fern.
53. **Glabrous**—without hairs or pubescence.
54. **Glaucous**—covered with a whitish "bloom."
55. **Habit**—the general appearance of a plant.
*56. **Head**—a short, dense inflorescence, frequently with ray flowers around the margins and *tubular* disk flowers inside.
57. **Herbaceous**—non-woody.
58. **Hirsute**—hairy.
59. **Humus**—incompletely decomposed organic materials in the soil.
60. **Hybrid**—the result of a cross between two parents differing in genetic composition.
61. **Hydrophyte**—water loving; a plant adapted to wet conditions; capable of growing in water.
62. **Imbricate**—overlapping vertically or spirally.
63. **Indehiscent**—fruits remaining closed at maturity.
64. **Inflorescence**—the arrangement of flowers in a cluster; a complete flower cluster.
65. **Internode**—the part of a stem between two nodes.
66. **Involucre**—a cycle of bracts subtending a flower or an inflorescence.
67. **Keel**—the two front, united petals of most leguminous flowers, e.g., pea.
*68. **Lanceolate**—lance-shaped, narrow and tapered at the ends, widening above the base and narrowed to the apex.
*69. **Legume**—dry, dehiscent fruit, single carpel, usually opening along both sutures.
70. **Lenticils**—small, corky areas on woody stems.
71. **Lenticular**—lens-shaped.
72. **Ligulate**—strap-shaped.
73. **Ligule**—a thin membrane at the top of the leaf sheath in the grasses.
74. **Lip**—one portion of an unequally divided corolla; often of different sizes or colors as in orchids.
75. **Monoecious**—having male and female flowers on the same plant.
76. **Morphology**—form, structure, and development.
77. **Needle**—the long, narrow leaf characteristic of the conifers, as pine and spruce.
78. **Node**—point on a stem from which a leaf or branch emerges.
*79. **Opposite** (leaves)—two leaves at each node, opposite each other.
*80. **Palmate**—palm-like, radiating outward from the base.
*81. **Panicle**—a compound raceme.
*82. **Papilionaceous** (corolla)—a pea-like flower, having a standard keel and wings.
83. **Pedicel**—the stem of a single flower.
84. **Peduncle**—the stem of an inflorescence.
85. **Perrenial**—a plant that lives from year to year and does not die after fruiting.
86. **Perfect** (flower)—having both stamens and carpels in the same flower.

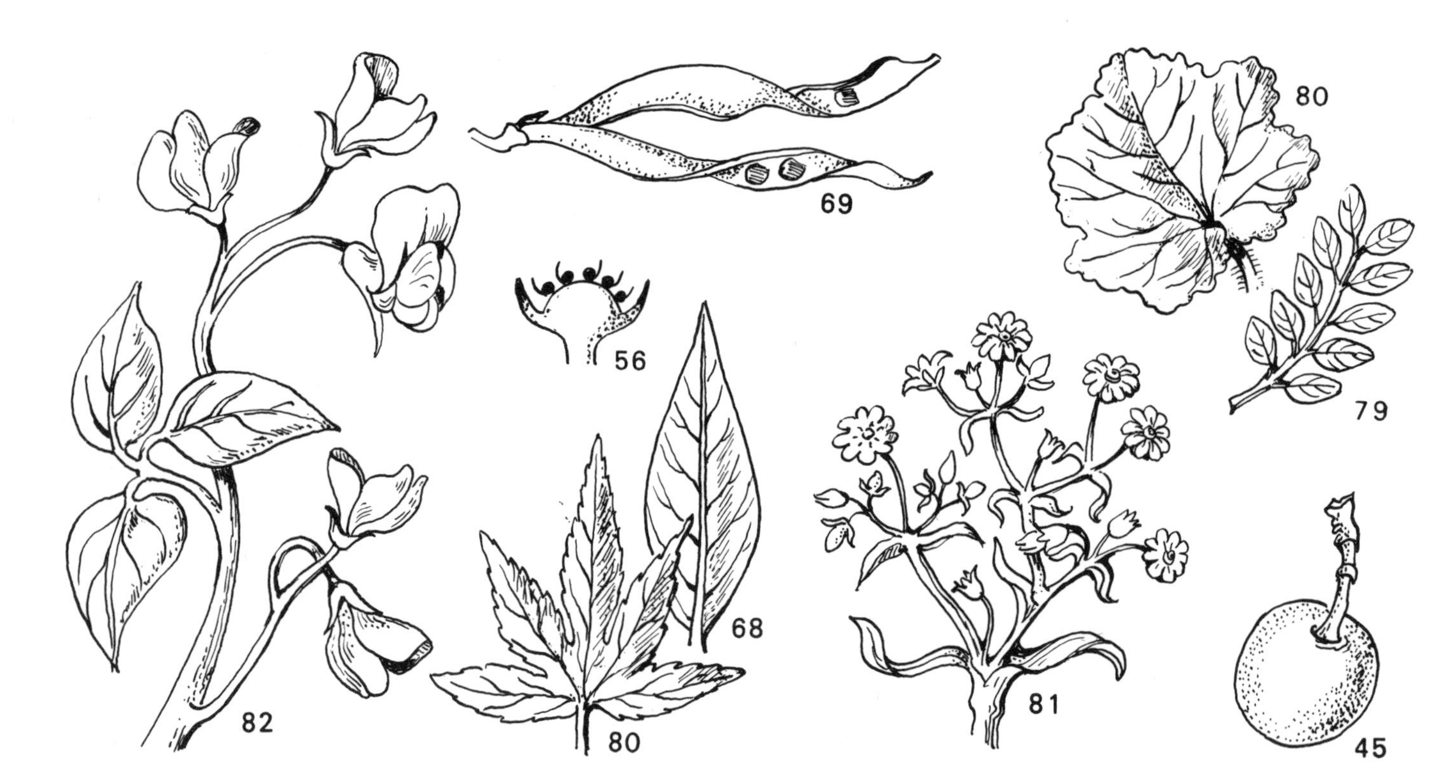

87. **Perianth**—the calyx and corolla.
88. **Persistent**—remaining attached.
89. **Petal**—one member of the corolla.
90. **Petiole**—the supporting stalk of the leaf blade.
91. **Pinnate**—separate leaflets arranged along a leaf stalk.
92. **Pistil**—the female reproductive parts of a flower, comprised of the stigma, style, and ovary.
*93. **Pome**—a fleshy, indehiscent fruit, with a leathery endocarp surrounding the seed, e.g., the apple.
94. **Pseudobulb**—thickened bulblike structure on leaves of epiphytic orchids.
95. **Pubescent**—covered with short hairs; downy.
96. **Raceme**—an elongated, indeterminate flower cluster with each floret on a pedicel.
97. **Rachis**—the axis of a spike.
98. **Receptacle**—the axis of a flower stalk bearing the floral parts.
99. **Reniform**—kidney-shaped.
100. **Reticulate**—as in a network of veins in a leaf.
101. **Rhizome**—an underground stem, usually horizontal, from which shoots and roots may develop.
102. **Rosette**—a cluster of leaves crowded on very short internodes.
103. **Rugose**—wrinkled.
104. **Sagittate**—arrow-shaped.
*105. **Samara**—a dry, indehiscent fruit having a wing, e.g., maple.
*106. **Scape**—a leafless flower stem arising from the soil.
107. **Schizocarp**—a dry, dehiscent fruit in which the carpels separate at maturation.
108. **Sepal**—a single member of the calyx.
109. **Septum**—a partition within an organ.
*110. **Serrate**—with sharp teeth and directed forward.
111. **Sessile**—without a stalk.
112. **Silique**—a dry, dehiscent fruit with two carpels separated by a septum.
113. **Sori**—spore masses on a fern.
*114. **Spadix**—a spike with a thick, fleshy axis, usually enveloped by a spathe.
*115. **Spathe**—a large bract or bracts surrounding an inflorescence.
116. **Spatulate**—spade-shaped; oblong with the basal end narrow.
*117. **Spike**—an inflorescence like a raceme except the florets are sessile to the peduncle.
118. **Stamen**—the male organ that bears the pollen.
119. **Standard** (in a papilionaceous corolla)—the large upper petal.
120. **Stigma**—the receptive part of the female organ.
121. **Stipule**—an appendage at the base of the petiole in some species.
122. **Stolon**—a prostrate stem that tends to root; sometimes called a runner.
123. **Style**—that part of the pistil connecting the stigma and the ovary.
124. **Succulent**—fleshy and juicy.
125. **Terrestrial**—plants growing in soil.
126. **Tomentose**—densely covered with hairs; woolly.
127. **Tuber**—underground storage organ; a stem with buds, e.g., the potato.
*128. **Umbel**—an indeterminate inflorescence in which the pedicels originate at about the same point on the peduncle and are about the same length, e.g., flowers of carrot.
*129. **Undulate**—a wavy surface.
130. **Variety**—a subdivision of a species, naturally occurring.
131. **Whorled**—leaves arranged in a circle around the stem.
132. **Wings**—(in a papilionaceous corolla)—the two side petals.
133. **Xerophyte**—a plant adapted to dry, arid conditions.

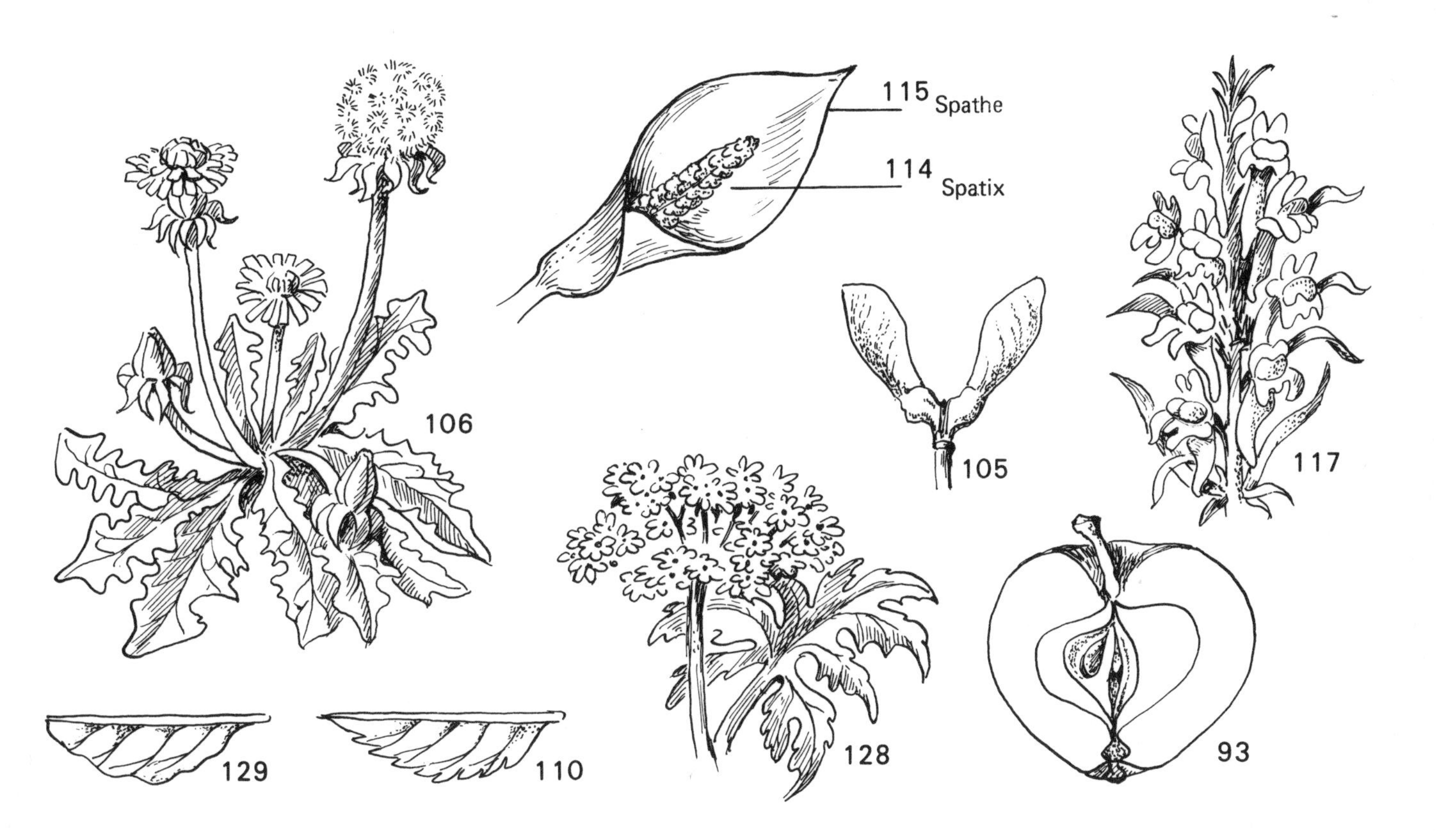

Index of plants mentioned

Small plants for edgings

Flowering plants for edgings are numerous; some are annual, some biennial and some perennial. They should be short and grow in clumps or clusters, in order not to leave empty spaces in the borders. They may have a height and a habit naturally suited to the purpose or they may be pruned and shaped to the desired height. The choice of species should be made in consideration of the flower color of the plants near the edging.

Among the most suitable small plants are the ageratum (*Ageratum coeruleum* and similar species), the English daisies *(Bellis perennis flore pleno),* the forget-me-nots *(Myosotis palustris* and *M. silvatica),* the rock cress, *(Aubrietia deltoidea),* the candytufts *(Iberis sempervirens* and similar species), the small begonias *(Begonia semperflorens)* the Sweet Williams *(Dianthus barbatus* and *Dianthus plumarius),* the lobelias (*Lobelia erinus* and others), and the *Convallaria majalis.*

For taller borders, some species of *Achillea, Amaranthus tricolor,* some *Cynoglossum, Iris germanica* and *I. florentina,* narcissus, nasturtiums, and some grasses of the *Phalaris* genus are very appropriate.

The ageratum includes a few species (*Ageratum coeruleum* or *A. conyzoides, A. Houstonianum, A. wendlandii:* Compositae family) all originating from Mexico, and grown since 1766 as cultivated plants.

Naturally, ageratum is a perennial plant but it is usually grown as an annual except in climates with no frost. It is a herbaceous plant 4 to 12 inches high, with a somewhat woody and branched habit. It has opposite leaves; the lower ones are oval and obtuse; the upper ones are narrower and rather rhomboidal; all of them are dull, light green, and with a toothed margin. The blossoms are in branched corymbs that create spots of light blue or lavender, and sometimes white: they have a velvety surface because of the stamens and have small, pointed petals. The seeds are small achenes with 5 corners, overtopped by tiny scales.

It is seeded in early spring under glass, transplanted to peat pots, and planted outdoors after all danger of frost is past. Distance between plants: 8 to 16 inches. It may be propagated by cuttings in the fall before frost.

The *Ageratum conyzoides* and the *A. wendlandii* have varieties with white clusters.

Aubrietia or sweet alyssum (*Aubrietia deltoidea:* Cruciferae family) is especially suited for edgings on limestone soil; it also grows in rock gardens very well. It originated from the Mediterranean regions and was introduced into gardens in 1823.

It is a small perennial plant, 4 to 8 inches tall, is branched and has alternate triangular, toothed leaves. The many flowers are white, pinkish-purple, or lilac; have four petals; and grow in thin clusters. The seeds are contained in oval siliques.

It is seeded in early spring, transplanted to peat pots, and planted outdoors after danger of frost is past at 6 to 12 inch spacings. It may be propagated by division in the early fall. It prefers light soil, sunny and not too moist locations. It flowers in spring, but both early and late varieties are known. There are also some varieties having smaller, but thicker flowers, some with brighter violet colors (var. *Tauricola*), with brighter purple colors (cultivar "Crimson King") and some others much darker (*A. hybrida* cv. "Dr. Mules" and others).

The forget-me-not, or myosotis, (*Myosotis palustris* and *M. sylvatica*) is classified into the Borraginaceae family. *M. palustris,* native of the northern latitudes, is mainly suited to moist locations, whereas *M. sylvatica* is suited for drier places, and it prefers semi-shady locations. They are sowed in June to August in the seed bed, and then to the garden in the fall or early spring. Spacing: 8 to 12 inches.

Forget-me-nots are well known for their tiny, blue flowers, having a yellow "throat" and four rounded petals.

Several species of candytufts may be grown (*Iberis amara, I. Jordanii, I. sempervirens,* and *I. umbellata:* Cruciferae family). The first three species mentioned have white or pinkish flowers, the fourth is violet. They are sparsely branched, 6 to 14 inches tall, with erect stalks carrying few narrow, pointed, small leaves with few large indentations. The flowers are sweet smelling, grouped in clusters in which the central florets are smaller and the outer ones have bigger petals. The *Iberis* are annuals or perennials, native to Europe, Asia Minor, and Africa. They are seeded in fall, grown over winter under protection, and planted outdoors in early spring, 8 to 16 inches apart.

---

1. *Myosotis palustris.*

2. Edging of *Aubrietia deltoidea.*

3

Wax begonias and other plants for color highlights

In flower beds, it is customary to arrange more or less large groupings of flowers. One of the small plants that serve this purpose well is wax begonia.

Begonia semperflorens (Begoniaceae family) is native to Brazil and has been known in gardening since 1828. It is herbaceous, perennial if not permitted to freeze, 6 to 14 inches tall, and multibranched. It has somewhat succulent leaves that are light green, often red-edged, bronze or coppery, and slightly indented. The flowers are in axillary inflorescences, and are pink, white, or red, having 4 or 5 petals with a yellow, thick tuft of stamens in the center.

The wax, or everblooming, begonia may be propagated by seed, and the seedlings will begin to flower when 3 to 4 months old. Seed sown in June will produce flowering plants for winter flowering. Sow seed in January or February for plants to be planted outdoors in the spring. This begonia may be reproduced by stem cutting, taken in the fall, using a cold greenhouse. Insert the cuttings into a light soil mixed with peat, or in sand or other propagated media. The plants then are kept in a temperate greenhouse for the winter. To obtain good cuttings, choose branches having a healthy bud at the base. Cold and windy locations are to be avoided. Distance to leave between the plants is from 4 to 8 inches.

The *Begonia semperflorens* cultivar "Schneetapete," or "snow-carpet," has white flowers and has an upright habit. The cultivars "Tausendschön" and "Rosanova" have scarlet or pink flowers clustered in thick groups. The "Red Pearl" is one of the shortest in stature, and has deep-red flowers, small stems, and few branches. Both Red Pearl and the cultivar "Primadonna" have red to red–brown leaves.

Other dwarf plants suitable for creating color highlights are violets, species of the *Viola* genus (Violaceae family), primarily *V. cornuta* and *V. odorata.* The latter is the violet well known for the perfume of its flowers. *Viola cornuta* is native to the Italian, French, and Spanish mountains, chiefly, of High Savoy and Pyrenees. As a garden plant it has been known since 1776. It is biennial or perennial, 5 to 10 inches tall, little branched and with alternate, oval, spatulate or almost heart-shaped, indented leaves. The flowers are irregular on long peduncles and have a corolla of about 1 inch across, with 5 petals; the two upper petals are larger and erect, the lowest one is wider. Color varies from a dark violet to a pale purple, or from white to a cream color to

4

5

6

7

bright yellow. The flowers of this species have some dark markings that spread out as a halo of lines on the petals beginning from the center on the flower. Each flower produces a three-valved capsule that contains many seeds.

The viola *(Viola odorata)* has lower height and smaller flowers in comparison to *V. cornuta.* It is also a perennial and a few varieties are known, including: the well-known Parma violet, with large, scented, dark-blue to purple colored flowers; the Russian violet, with darker flowers on longer stems; and the four-seasons violet, which blossoms continuously. Available also are cultivars having white flowers, hybrids, and related species with blue flowers *(Viola mumbyana)* or yellow flowers *(Viola vilmoriniana).*

Violets and violas may be propagated by seeds, by stolons, or by division. Seeding is done July-August and seedlings transplanted in September or October for spring bloom.

Another good plant is the alyssum "Basket-of-Gold" (*Alyssum saxatile:* Brassicaceae family), which has golden-yellow flowers and is ideal for contrast with species having violet, blue, red, or purple flowers. Seed is sown from June to July in a light soil mixture and the young plants are transplanted in the fall or early spring.

3. Flower bed of *Begonia semperflorens.*
4. Close-up of *B. semperflorens* flower.
5. *Begonia semperflorens,* cultivar "Rosanova."
6. *Viola cornuta* (Horned Violet).
7. *Alyssum saxatile,* cultivar "Basket-of-Gold."

8

Portulacas (sun-plants)

The portulaca (*Portulaca grandiflora:* Portulacaceae family) is a small plant that originated in Brazil and Argentina.

It is perennial but is killed by frost. The plants are only 3 to 8 inches high, are spreading and multibranched. Portulaca is well adapted for use in beds, borders, edges, hanging baskets, and rock gardens. It has succulent stems and leaves. The stems are reddish-purple, the leaves are needle shaped, dark green, and glabrous or thinly velveted. The flowers are large, isolated, and open completely in direct sunlight; in their simple forms, they are composed of 4 to 6 silky, oval-rounded, slightly heart-shaped petals. The flowers may be of various colors, from white to a cream color to yellow, from pink to dark lilac, and from red to bright carmine, with all intermediate shades. It is seeded in early spring, outdoors, and the plants are thinned to stand 5 to 10 inches apart. Seed may also be sown earlier inside and transplanted outdoors after danger of frost is past. It prefers a well-drained soil and locations exposed to the sun.

There are some kinds having double flowers that are very pretty; culture is the same as the single ones.

Portulacas blossom continuously from about July to frost. The heterogeneity of their colors provides beds and edgings with a charming mosaic effect.

8. Bed of *Portulaca grandiflora.*
9-12. Individual flowers of portulaca.

9

10

11

12

13

Gazania

The Gazania (*Gazania splendens,* Com-positae family) is probably a hybrid between *Ga-zania Pavonia* and *G. Uniflora* and comes from the Cape of Good Hope.

It is a small plant with a prostrate habit and has both upright and spreading, short stems. The leaves are sessile, almost persistent, oppo-site, tapered, 2 to 4 inches long, dark green on the upper side and grayish-white below. Th flowers are large, solitary blossoms with a diam-eter of 1 to 2 inches, and are similar to larg daisies, having a large ligules with purplish black or whitish spots at the base.

It blossoms copiously from May to October It is sown indoors in the early winter and planted out after frost danger is past. It prefer warm climate, full sun, and loose soil; it is par-ticularly indicated for gardens in the south. I can be propagated by cuttings in August and September.

Other species are also used: *Gazania rigen* var. *citrina* has flowers with yellow rays and greenish crown; *G. longiscapa,* has very large blossoms. A cultivar with variegated leaves i rare and not vigorous. A number of cultivar having flowers ranging from yellow to orange to even red are grown as *Gazania Hybrida.*

14

13. Bed of *Gazania splendens.*

14, 15. *Gazania longiscapa.*

16. *Gazania rigens* var. *citrina.*

19

Primroses

Primroses (*Primula* genus: Primulaceae family) include a large number of species, some of which grow well outdoors. We will only mention here the *Primula sinensis* and *P. obconica* which are suited only for potting, but call attention to the cowslips *(Primula veris)* and two garden species: *Primula polyantha* and *P. hortensis. P. polyantha* is related to the wild *P. acaulis,* of woods and shores, having yellow flowers. *P. hortensis* is related to *P. veris* and to *P. auricula,* which grow wild in the mountains.

At any rate, the well known *Primula veris* grows 2 to 6 inches high, is perennial, and without a distinct stem it has tufted appearance. The leaves, all basal and arranged as a rosette, are large (2 to 4 inches), oblong-spatulate, rugose, with indented margins, and generally have a festive green color. In the center of the rosette of leaves, the flowers are produced; they are numerous and tightly gathered as in a nosegay. The floret is round and has 5 petals. The calyx is slightly swollen with 5 ridges. Flower color varies greatly among the many different cultivars, being yellow in wild *Primula vulgaris.* Flowers may be unicolored, or bicolored with either a yellow center or one that is at least lighter than the rest of the corolla, which may be pink, purple, red, violet, or blue. The plant produces ovoid capsules with a large number of seeds.

Primula is a sturdy plant, suitable for edgings, thickets, and rock gardens. It is sown in spring or early summer in the seed bed in the shade, transplanted into loose-textured soil in early fall or in the following spring; distance between the plants: 6 to 10 inches. It may be propagated by dividing the clumps, best done in the summer. It does not require a special culture or soil.

A large number of cultivars with double or single flowers are available; those with bicolored flowers are also known as "owl's eyes."

17-21. *Primula vulgaris* flowers, illustrating the interesting range of color.

22

23

Pansies

The pansy includes many cultivars all derived genetically from *Viola tricolor* (Violaceae family), a native of Europe, the little white, yellow, and blue-purplish violet of the fields. The most commonly grown pansy today is either *Viola Tricolor* var. *hortensis,* or *V. tricolor* var. *grandiflora.*

It is an annual or biennial plant (occasionally perennial), 2 to 12 inches high with an open habit. It has oval-lanceolate, indented leaves each bearing two finger-like stipules. The nonodorous flowers may be as large as 2½ inches in diameter; they are irregular and with a posterior spur, and have 5 rounded velvety, unicolored, or variously bordered or tinted petals, with markings or spots. The throat of the corolla is usually yellow. The range in flower color is quite wide, from pink, to red, to blue, to purple, to almost black. The numerous, tiny seeds are contained in a three-valved, dehiscent capsule.

The pansy is a sturdy plant that is used for edges, bedding purposes, hanging baskets, and even for cut flowers. It should not have much shade or dampness. It is sown outdoors from July to August in the seed bed in light soil, and the young plants are transplanted from September to October to the garden or to a cold frame (distance left between plants: 6 to 12 inches). It may also be propagated by division.

Pansies are subject to several diseases, including powdery mildew and violet rust. These diseases may be controlled with appropriate fungicides that are available at garden centers.

Among the well-known kinds are the Swiss Giants: Alpenglow, rich cardinal shades; Berna, violet blue; Coronation, golden yellow; Swiss Blue, medium blue; Swiss Orange, orange to golden yellow; Rhinegold, yellow with dark blotch and Raspberry Rose, a pink. In addition to these, there are many excellent mixtures such as Oregon Giants, Roggli Swiss Giants, Steeles Jumbo, and Butterfly hybrids.

22–26. Flowers of some of the most interesting pansy cultivars.

24

25

26

Cinerarias

The cineraria (*Senecio hybridus=Cineraria hybrida:* Asteraceae or Compositae family) is developed from the *Senecio cruentus* which it resembles; it is native of the Canary Islands and it has been used in gardens since 1777.

It is a biennial plant (perennial if protected); it is 10 to 20 inches high, erect and branched at the top. It has large, heart-shaped, variously toothed and dull leaves that are also velvety; they are rugose and light green on top. The flowers are in clusters of large heads that resemble large daisies with wide petals. The plant flowers profusely. The flower heads have a central reddish, dark-brown or purple-violet disk and rays of different colors that range from lilac-pink, to red, to violet to blue, with very intense and bright gradations. There are many cultivars with bicolored flowers, usually having a light central crown.

The seeds are brown, oblong achenes. Some cultivars with tubulous ligules that are improperly called double-flowered cinerarias, also exist; and there are some that actually have double flowers.

Seeds are sown from June through August for flowering in the greenhouse in the winter, then transplanted into well-drained pots as soon as the first true leaf appears. In southern locations they can be sown outdoors. For the cultivars in which one wants to maintain any particular characteristics, like double flowered ones, the propagation is by cuttings using basal branches with buds. Cinerarias bloom from winter to early spring.

Cinerarias are subject to wilting and leaf browning caused by the bread mold organism, and to powdery mildew. The former disease shows up first as pale spots on the leaves, which become yellow and then brown, and, in moist conditions will be covered with a gray mold; often the plants wilt and die. It is advisable to ventilate the plants if they are in the greenhouse or under glass, to reduce the applications of nitrogen fertilizer if they have been excessive, and to treat the plants with fungicides. Soil disinfection also gives good results. Powdery mildew usually develops during periods of cool, moist nights, and can be checked by application of of suitable fungicides.

Related species include *Senecio grandiflorus* introduced to Europe from Mexico in 1844, having yellow flower heads, and from which some taxonomists believe *Cineraria hybrida* is derived; *Senecio pulcher,* from Argentina, with flowers having a yellow disk and lilac rays; and *S. Petasitis* from South America, with golden flowers.

27

28

29

30

31

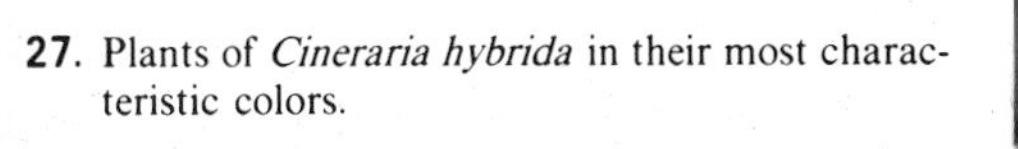

27. Plants of *Cineraria hybrida* in their most characteristic colors.

28–30. Examples of colors in some cultivars.

31. Close-up of a cineraria blossom, showing detail.

32

Calendulas, or pot marigolds

The calendula (so named because it blooms any month of the year) is also called pot marigold and is derived from the original botanical species named *Calendula officialis* (Compositae family). Native of Southern Europe, it has been cultivated for decorative purposes since 1542.

It is an annual herbaceous plant, 8 to 15 inches tall that has a particular, aromatic fragrance. It is erect and branched at the top. The leaves are alternate, rather thick, glandulous, and lightly sticky, have an oblong shape and a light green color. The blossoms consist of large flowers (up to 2½ inches in diameter) that are solitary, apical, and contained in a global rosette; the tubular flowers of the central disk are yellow, orange, or brownish. The ray flowers are very numerous and range in color from light yellow to bright orange.

The seeds are oblong, curved achenes, and are dark yellow.

Calendulas may be used in flower beds for edging and for beds or hanging baskets. They are very suitable for use as cut flowers. They bloom during summer and fall.

They can be sowed indoors or in a greenhouse in the seed bed from March through April and transplanted outdoors in April or May. It is also possible to sow them directly outdoors. They require rich soil and a sunny location. The calendula has been used by herbalists, since its blooms have anti-emetic and wound-healing properties; the juice of the leaves and stems extracted at the time of full bloom has been used against warts.

Variations other than those for color are known. The double calendulas have attracted favorable attention. Multibranching cultivars form plants shaped like bouquets. The two most important cultivars are "Ball's Gold" with yellow flowers and "Ball's Orange" with bright, red-orange flowers.

33

34

32. Bed of *Calendula officialis.*

33. A flower of the cultivar "Ball's Gold" showing some detail.

34. Blossoms of the cultivar "Ball's Orange."

Marigolds

Marigolds are characterized by their strong fragrance, unpleasant to many people. They are of two species: *Tagetes patula,* also called French Marigold and *T. erecta* also known by the common name of Aztec or African Marigold (Compositae family).

They are annual plants introduced from Mexico to Europe during the Sixteenth Century. The species differ both in height and shape of the flowers. *Tagetes patula* is from 5 to 20 inches tall, erect and bushy, with mostly opposite compound dark leaves. The blossoms are either single or double flowered, and from 1 to 2 inches in diameter. The disk flowers are tufted and yellow or orange. The ray flowers vary greatly in number and are yellow to reddish, or spotted with purple-brown toward the center of the blossom. Some cultivars are basically orange, yellow, brown, or purple in the center. The ligules are either flat or tubular. Some dwarf cultivars are particularly suitable for edging.

Tagetes erecta is taller (20 to 40 inches) and has larger flowers (2 to 3 inches in diameter) that are yellow (*T. erecta flore pleno,* cultivar "Yellow Supreme"), or double golden or orange (*T. erecta flore pleno* cultivar "Guinea Gold"). It is suitable for beds and as cut flowers. In both species the seeds are elongate, black, shiny achenes.

Marigolds are very rugged, and prefer sunny locations; they may be seeded in early spring, transplanted to peat pots and planted outside after danger of frost is past. Distance to leave between the plants is from 10 to 15 inches for *Tagetes patula* and from 12 to 24 inches for *T. erecta.* They bloom from June to October and in the southern regions even during winter.

Related species include *Tagetes tenuifolia* or Indian carnation, and *T. lucida:* both were introduced from Mexico during the 18th Century.

Among the cultivars of *T. patula* are *T. patula nana flore pleno* cv. "Light Lemon yellow," with double yellow flowers, and cv. "Robert Beist" also double, but with red-brown to purple colors. The cultivar "Harmony" has a big tuft of yellow twisted flowers in the center, with a crown of wide purple ligules around the edge; cultivar "Naughty Marietta" is simple flowered having wide, yellow rays with a big purple spot at the base of each. Cultivar "Flash" is also simple-flowered, but the rays are reddish-brown.

Tagetes tenuifolia, var. *pumila* is a dwarf plant with small leaves and tiny blossoms that are solitary and completely yellow.

---

35. Bed of *Tagetes tenuifolia* var. *pumila.*

36. Blossom of *T. patula* cultivar "Naughty Marietta."

37. Bed of *T. patula flore pleno* hybrid.

38. Blossom of *T. patula flore pleno* cultivar "Robert Beist."

39. Blossom of *T. erecta flore pleno* cultivar "Guinea Gold."

40 41

Calceolarias and nasturtiums

These two plants have great ornamental qualities and are interesting for the unusual shape of their flowers, extremely different in the two species and perhaps only associated by their colors, which range from all gradations of yellow and orange to red and purple.

The calceolaria (*Calceolaria hybrida:* Scrophulariaceae family) is genetically linked to *C. integrifolia, C. arachnoidea, C. corimbosa* and *C. crenatiflora.* A native of Chile, it has been used in gardens since 1822.

Calceolaria is perennial if not exposed to frost, but is grown as an annual. It is 8 to 15 inches high, sometimes reaching 25 inches, with erect and sparsely branched stems; the leaves are alternate or opposite, oval or oblong with a winged stalk, wrinkled and rugose above, wavy and toothed. Its flowers characteristically exhibit the shapes of a swollen kidney and a small flattened bag, due to the two lips of the corolla: the upper one is smaller and shaped like a hood and the lower one is expanded, swollen, and very wide, like the labellum of some orchids. The flowers may have one color or be variously dotted or spotted. The seeds, grain-shaped, are numerous inside capsules. Blossoming occurs in late winter and spring.

42

The calceolarias are propagated by seed, which is sown from May to September in a fine soil; the young plants are transplanted when they are large enough to handle. Certain kinds are propagated by cuttings in a temperate greenhouse in September; they will have to spend the winter in a cool greenhouse, and flower in the spring. Distance between plants: 10 to 16 inches. Cuttings are made with branches that are still herbaceous, rooted in sandy, acid soil. The cultivars are unicolored, striped, spotted and "tigered."

Hybrids with other species are grown, including *Calceolaria fruticohybrida* (derived from *C. amplexicaulis.*) *C. alba* has white flowers. *C. polyrrhiza* is a perennial, dwarf species, 3 to 5 inches high, which is a native of Patagonia and is used for beds and rock gardens.

They are subject to being infested by aphids and red spider mites which should be controlled by appropriate insecticides.

Nasturtiums (*Tropaeolum majus*) and their variations belong to the Tropaeolaceae family. They originated in Peru.

T. majus is annual, with a prostrate habit, and with dwarf or semi-dwarf cultivars.

The plant is smooth and waxy; the leaves are round with the petiole attached at the center of the blade. The large flowers have a corolla formed by 5 wide, free, oval, petals with a thin and ciliated throat, and with a spur in the back. Color, always velvety, varies from yellow to orange to red and to brownish-purple. The seeds are large, kidney-shaped, and dark yellow. The buds and the fruits are used, like capers, to make pickles; the flowers are quite edible and are used to brighten salads.

Nasturtiums are seeded in February and March indoors for subsequent transplanting or they may be seeded directly in the bed after danger of frost is over. They should be planted or thinned to a 12- to 18-inch spacing. Special types, such as the double-flowered cultivars, may be propagated by cuttings.

Related species include *Tropaeolum minus,* with smaller, orange or red flowers (cultivar "King of Tom Thumb"), *T. peregrinum,* with very small, yellow flowers and lobed leaves, *T. peltophorum* with large orange flowers.

The cultivar "Gyldenskar" is one of the most beautiful with its golden, overdoubled flowers.

40, 41. Appearance of *Tropaeolum majus* in blossom.

42. *Calceolaria hybrida.*

43

44

Petunias

The garden petunia (*Petunia hybrida*) is derived from the two species *Petunia nyctaginiflora* and *P. violacea* (Solanaceae family).

The pentunia is a perennial, although it is grown as an annual. It grows 10 to 20 inches tall, has an erect but disorderly habit, and often its branches fall down. The whole plant is light grayish-green, and velvety. The leaves are alternate or opposite, rounded or oval. Flowers are large, trumpet-shaped, and tubular with united petals having an expanded and circular edge, observation of which allows one to distinguish the 5 joined petals. Flower color varies from white to red to purple to a dark violet. They may be of a single, uniform color or with spots that often design a star. Some cultivars are single, some are double; some have a curled corolla that resembles a carnation. The seeds, globular and tiny, are in an oval capsule.

Petunias bloom all summer, generally from May to October. They are seeded in early spring, transplanted to peat pots, and planted outside at a spacing of 12 to 20 inches after danger of frost is past. Plants with double flowers are propagated by cuttings in order to maintain their characteristics. Such propagation is done in spring inside pots under glass and in not too sunny locations. They require little moisture: in fact, excessive water will cause yellowing and death.

Among the most interesting cultivars are "Himmelsroschen" with single flowers having a bright pink color with a white throat; the "Bla Vidunder" with lavender flowers; *P. hybrida* var. *violacea* with a dark violet corolla; "Satellite," with purple petals and a white star having a narrow point; "Glitters," similar to Satellite but with larger white points; "Canadian Wonder" with a large, crinkled, purple corolla and with a throat veined with violet-brown.

43. Bed of *Petunia hybrida* with red flowers.

44. Cultivar "Satellite."

45. Cultivar "Glitters."

46, 47. Cultivar with crinkled flowers.

45

46

47

48

49

50

51

52

Verbenas

The colorful garden Verbena, *Verbena hybrida* (Verbenaceae family) may be derived from such American species as *Verbena chamaedryfolia* from Tropical regions, *V. incisa* from Panama, *V. phlogiflora* from Brazil, and *V. teucrioides* from Chile. All the species cited and the hybrids have been cultivated since the early 19th century.

The verbena is a perennial but is normally grown as an annual. It is erect, with branches often prostrate, and branched at the top of the plant. The leaves are opposite, oval to oblong, small and indented. The flowers are scented and grouped in large numbers into umbrella-shaped clusters, similar to round bouquets. They have a united corolla, about ½ inch in diameter that is round and has 5 petals. Color varies from white to pink to red, to blue to purple, and even to brown and gray. They may be uniform in color, variegated or striped. The throat is always white or yellowish-green and always lighter than the petals. The seeds are small, cylindrical, and wrinkled.

Verbenas, blossom from June to October, and may be used well in edgings, mass plantings, and beds. They may also be grown in pots and the flowers used for cutting. Sow seeds in August to September outdoors, transplant seedlings into pots, and keep over winter in a cool greenhouse. Then when the plants begin to flower, transfer them outdoors. Distance to leave between plants is from 6 to 12 inches. Seeds may also be sown in February and March in the greenhouse, the seedlings later transplanted, and the young plants set outdoors in May. The direct propagation by cuttings in the winter and spring is possible, using fresh, mature herbaceous branches, or in the fall with selected cuttings from plants outdoors. Verbenas prefer well prepared garden soil and need a sunny location.

A large number of cultivars are available, which are classified into two groups: Italian, which are unicolored, variegated flowers with a large throat of a different color.

Verbena hybrida, cv. *candidissima* has white flowers and a dwarf habit, the cultivar "Defiance" is bright red, "Dannebrog" has red flowers and a large white and shaded throat, and "Royal Blue" has dark, violet-blue flowers.

Among the related ornamental species are *Verbena canadensis,* (= *V. Aubletia*) with dark red flowers; *V. pulchella* and *V. tenera* with lilac-violet flowers; and *V. rigida,* lilac or blue-violet forming a pyramidal cluster and having wrinkled leaves.

48-51. Some cultivars of *Verbena hybrida.*

52. Hybrid of *Verbena chamaedrifolia* with velvet red flowers.

54

Snapdragons

Snapdragons (*Antirrhinum majus:* Scrophulareaceae family) are among the most well-known flowers and are peculiar because of their large tubular and swollen corollas whose throat, when the walls of the corolla are pressed together, opens up wide. In Europe it is sometimes called the "Mouth of the Lion." Snapdragons originated in Southern Europe. They have been cultivated since at least the 16th Century.

It may be an annual, biennial, or perennial, grows 12 to 30 inches tall, is erect and not greatly branched. The leaves are opposite or alternate, lanceolate, narrow, and entire. The flowers, blooming in spring and summer, are numerous and grow on an erect and terminal cluster. The corolla is united and ranges from white to yellow to light pink, or salmon to red to copper and even to reddish-violet; it also generally has a yellow spot at the opening of the throat. Seeds are small, brown and numerous, and develop in a capsule.

Snapdragons are sown in a greenhouse or indoors in February or March for planting outdoors in the spring; distance between the plants should be from 12 to 20 inches. They can also be sown outdoors from April to May. To flower in a greenhouse in the winter, sow in July to October. 16 to 18 weeks are required from sowing seed to bloom. The propagation of double or selected kinds is possible by cuttings. The snapdragon prefers slightly acid soil and sun.

It is a sturdy plant, having dwarf, semi-dwarf and tall types. The dwarf and semi-dwarf types may be grown in beds or rock gardens; the tall types do well in beds or for cut flowers. There are also cultivars of bicolored, shaded, or spotted flowers.

There are many interesting cultivars, varying in flower color and habit or growth. New F_1 hybrid types are available either in separate or mixed colors. Popular types are: Rocket Snapdragons, 30 to 36 inches tall; Floral Carpet Snapdragons, 6 to 8 inches; Tetra Snapdragons, 24 to 30 inches; Butterfly Snapdragons, with open-face florets, and doubles.

53, 54. Groups of snapdragons in blossom, showing the beauty of mixed colors.

55, 56. Close-up of snapdragon flowers.

Wallflowers, stocks, and nemesias

Mathiola incana (Stocks) and *Cheiranthus Cheiri* (Wallflowers) are natives of Mediterranean Europe (probably the islands of Greece) or of the Middle East. Cultivated since 1583, varieties with double flowers have since been developed. Both belong to the crucifer family.

M. incana is an annual, biennial, or perennial plant, 12 to 30 inches tall, and is branched at the top. The column stock is unbranched. It has alternate, oblong, narrow, entire leaves, silvery-green, and velvety. Its flowers are large and either single with 4 petals, or more commonly double. They are brightly colored in pink-lilac, white, purple or yellow, and are very fragrant. The seeds are disk-shaped, reddish, winged, and develop in long, cylindrical siliques.

C. Cheiri is quite similar to *M. incana;* the plant is dark green and the flowers are yellow or orange; they may also be unicolored, or striped or spotted with red or brown. They are mostly single and bloom in the spring.

They are sown in January through April under glass and are transplanted a first time when the plants have 3 or 4 leaves. Seed may be sown in October or November and young plants carried over the winter in protected frames. The cultivars of *Cheiranthus* can be considered perennial plants; those of *Matthiola* may be biennial or perennial. *M. incana* var. *annua* is annual and blooms about 2 ½ months after sowing. Both dwarf and tall varieties exist, as well as some that bloom in fall the year following sowing.

Wallflowers prefer a sandy soil with high pH, and grow best in full sun.

There is also *Cheiranthus Allionii* (=*Erysimum asperum*) which grows rapidly and has small, single, yellow flowers.

Nemesias, *Nemesia floribunda, N. strumosa, N. versicolor,* and their hybrids (Scrophulariaceae family) were introduced from Africa and Austrialia in about 1830. They are annuals, 10 to 15 inches tall, and branched from the base. They have opposite leaves; the lower ones are oval and the upper ones narrow. The flowers are about 1 inch in diameter with a round but slightly irregular corolla. They are whitish, shaded, and rayed in yellow and violet or they may be yellow, red or purple, and dotted or streaked. The seeds are small and winged, and are in a bivalved capsule.

These plants are suitable for borders and beds and blossom from May to August. Seed is sown in September; seedlings are transplanted to a protected frame or cool greenhouse for the winter and planted in March or April outdoors. It is also possible to sow them indoors in February or March and later transplant them outside, thinning to a distance of from 6 to 12 inches. They require light soil and good sunny locations.

These three types of plants grow and flower best in cool climates or in a greenhouse plant where the night temperatures do not exceed 60°F.

57. *Cheiranthus Cheiri.*

58, 60. *Nemesia floribunda.*

59. Bed of *Cheiranthus Allionii.*

57 58 59 60

61

weet williams and garden pinks

Sweet Williams (*Dianthus barbatus;* Caryo-
hyllaceae family), have been cultivated since
bout 1750, and are native to Eurasia, from Italy
ɔ Bulgaria, and Central Russia to China.

It is biennial or perennial, 12 to 20 inches tall,
rect with strong stems and opposite, lanceolate,
ark green leaves. The flowers grow in a corymb.
he corollas are regular, round (about 1 inch in
iameter) and are formed by 5 triangular petals
aving a very narrow throat and a toothed mar-
in. Colors vary from white to pink to dark pur-
le; sometimes the flowers are unicolored, but
ıore often they have a darker rayed halo. Some
re "eyed," spotted or streaked.

Sweet Williams are used in flower beds or
dges and can be cut for house decorations. They
loom in April to July, during their second year.
hey are sown in July to August in the seed bed,
ransplanted to a protected area in September-
)ctober and to the garden in the spring. In mild
limates they may be transplanted to the garden
ı the fall. Distance between plants: 12 to 20
nches.

Cultivars with double flowers are available
nd have a very decorative effect for flowery
arpets.

Garden Pinks, also known by many other
ames, is *Dianthus plumarius.* This plant is
robably native to the Orient and Southeastern
urope. It is perennial, but it is commonly culti-
ated as an annual. It has a dwarf bushy habit,
eaching a height of about 8 inches. It is multi-
ranched and the stems and leaves are waxy and
ght green. The leaves are opposite and lanceolate.

The fragrant flowers are white, pink or purple,
and have narrow, triangular petals with fringed
margins.

They bloom throughout the summer and are
excellent for borders and for rock gardens. Both
single- and double-flowered types are available,
some unicolored or streaked or dotted. The culture is similar to that for the Sweet William.

61-64. Beds and single plants of *Dianthus barbatus* showing the variety of color.

62

63

64

65

68

Daisies

These are common plants belonging to several species of Compositae family having in common the characteristic shape of the flower head: narrow rays extending from a white or yellow central disk.

Chrysanthemum maximum is originally from the Pyrenees and the horticultural forms are known as Shasta Daisy. It is perennial, has an erect and bushy habit, 20 to 30 inches tall, and has oblong and toothed leaves. The flowers are 2 to 3 inches in diameter with a yellow disk and white rays, sometimes on two rows. It is used in mass plantings and its flowers can be cut. It needs a rich soil and a sunny location.

Chrysanthemum frutescens, the Marguerite or Paris Daisy, is native to the Canary Islands and has been grown since about 1700. It is perennial, bushy, and grows about 20 inches high. It has oblong leaves, toothed or deeply pinnate. Its flowers are smaller than *C. maximum.* Cultivars with double and with yellow flowers are available. It may be grown from seeds with adequate protection but is customarily propagated by cuttings. It blooms from late spring until fall in temperate climates and it is very ornamental as a specimen plant.

Other daisies with nice flowers include: *Chrysanthemum coronarium* with laciniate-toothed leaves and yellow or white, mostly double flower heads; *C. segetum* with yellow flowers; *C. coccineum* with white and double flowers (White Queen Mary) or with carmine rays (James Kelway) or pink rays (Eileen May Robinson).

English Daisy is the common name of *Bellis perennis,* a familiar plant in European meadows having shaded white ligules. Normally single flowered in nature, there are double-flowere cultivars (*Bellis hybrida flore pleno,*) with white pink, or carmine flower heads, and some kind with globular heads. It is perennial, native t Europe. It blooms from April to June, it is 2 t 5 inches high and has a basal rosette of spatulate toothed leaves. The flower heads are single, api cal, on peducles without leaves. It is used fo edgings and as a bedding plant. It is seeded i July or August and planted outdoors in fall o early spring. It is also possible to seed it directly Especially valuable cultivars are propagated b division.

65, 66. Flower bed and flower head of *Chrysanth mum maximum.*

67. *Bellis perennis flore pleno.*

68. *Chrysanthemum frutescens.*

71

72

Asters and gaillardias

Asters are species of the *Aster* genus (Compositae family). They are herbaceous, tall and bushy, and either with numerous flower heads in a delicate violet color (purple asters), or with large single flowers, sometimes white and similar to daisies. Purple asters include: *Aster Amellus* having a yellow disk and lilac-blue rays; *Aster novae-angliae* and *A. novi-belgii* with white, pink, lilac, or purple rays and yellow disks.

A. Amellus is indigenous to the Middle East and the Caucasus; the other two, to North America. They grow from 3 to 6 feet tall, are bushy, with lanceolate, entire and shiny leaves. They are useful planted in groups and for cut flowers. They may be seeded in February indoors and transplanted outdoors; but the usual propagation is by division.

Aster Amellus cultivars "Wonder of Staffa" and "Kobold" have violet flowers, "Sonia" is pink, and "October" is violet. *Aster alpinus* is the dwarf Alpine aster that has varieties among which var. *superbus* has large violet-lilac rays.

An *Aster hybridus* derived from *A. novi-belgii* has very small leaves and numerous, double lilac-red flowers.

The so-called Chinese Asters are either single or double flowered and belong to the species *Callistephus chinensis.*

The gaillardia, *Gaillardia pulchella* or *G. aristata* (Compositae family), is of North American origin. They may be annual, biennial, or perennial. They grow about 15 inches tall, have oblong leaves on the higher part of the plant, and irregularly lobed and toothed leaves on the lower. The flower heads, shaped like daisies, have reddish-yellow disks and rays of golden-yellow at the periphery and purple at the base. It is a robust plant, seeded in spring, transplanted to pots, and planted outdoors in April-May. Variety *grandiflora* is the most beautiful.

69. An *Aster* with white rays.

70. *A. Amellus.*

71. A group of double "Chinese Asters."

72. Group of *Coreopsis tinctoria*—an annual species (see page 35).

Centaureas

The most common of the centaureas is the Cornflower or Bachelor's Button (*Centaurea Cyanus:* Compositae family). Cultivars with white, pink, lilac, and blue flowers have been developed. The cornflower is an annual or biennial herbaceous plant, originating in Europe and the Middle East. The plant is quite common, is very sturdy, and is used for mass plantings and cut flowers.

It is seeded in August or September in mild areas, directly where it will flower; otherwise it can be sowed indoors in February or March and transplanted outdoors in April when the plants have reached a good level of development at a spacing of from 12 to 18 inches. It is also possible to sow them directly outdoors in spring, thinning the plants as needed. The cornflower will also reseed itself. It requires loose soil and a sunny location.

Its roots and flower heads are sometimes used by the herbalist for making extracts used as eyedrops; it also has an anticough action.

Many related species are also very ornamental such as: *Centaurea oxylepis,* which has pink flowers with finely-fringed rays; *C. americana* (Basket Flower) with lilac flowers; *C. moschata* (Sweet Sultan) with yellow, fragrant flowers; and *C. macrocephala* with yellow blossoms.

Centaura montana (Mountain Bluet) has much larger blossoms in blue and pink-lilac. Native to mountain meadows, where it blossoms from May to July, it is possible to grow it in gardens where it can have fall bloom as well as spring flowers.

73, 74. *Centaurea Cyanus.*

75. *C. oxylepis.*

76. *C. macrocephala.*

73

78

;osmos and other asteraceae

Cosmos, *Cosmos bipinnatus* (Compositae amily) is native to Mexico. They are annuals hat bloom from July to October, and grow from to 6 feet tall, with erect, branched stems. .eaves are opposite, bipinnate, with very narrow eaflets that make the plant bushy. The flowers .re 2 to 4 inches in diameter, have a central 'ellow disk, and rays of not too many ligules hat are wide and toothed at their tips. The color f the flowers ranges from white to pink to red o purple.

It is a very suitable plant for mass plantings or naking temporary hedges and for cut flowers. It s seeded in the spring outdoors. Earlier bloom an be obtained by seeding indoors in early pring and transplanting outside. Distance be-ween plants should be from 15 to 24 inches. Cosmos prefers rich soils and sunny locations.

Other than the kinds already mentioned on hese pages, other Compositaes are grown, in-luding: the yellow Anthemis *(Anthemis tinc-oria);* other species of *Chrysanthemums* (for example, *C. carinatum*) that are discussed on pages 49 and 50: the Coreopsis with yellow flower heads (*Coreopisis lancellata,* or *Coreopsis tinctoria*) with yellow and brown-purple colors. Dahlias, rudbeckias and sunflowers are also discussed elsewhere.

These plants do not have particular requirements and may be grown in the same way as daisies.

79

77-79. Various cultivars of *Cosmos bipinnatus.*

80. *Chrysanthemum carinaturm* (cultivar Lord Beaconsteel).

80

77

81

82

83

84

85

Peonies and buttercups

Peonies and buttercups belong to the same family Ranunculaceae.

The peony *(Paeonia albiflora)* is a beautiful plant originating in Siberia and China. It is perennial, 2 to 3 feet tall, with fleshy thickened roots. It has many stems, giving the plant a bushy appearance. Leaves have three to six leaflets, each small and oval. The flowers are slightly fragrant; they are large, double or single, white shaded with pink, yellowish, or bright pink to carmine. Flowers consist of many rounded unequal petals that often are wavy or laciniate. In the center, in some cultivars, a tuft of stamens with yellow anthers surrounds an ovary of three carpels that will contain 2 to 5 large round seeds resembling small peas.

Peonies are normally propagated by division. They can be grown from seed, but do not then produce blossoms for about 5 years or more. They are suited for mass plantings, and isolated plants can have an aesthetic effect if planted at least 3 feet apart.

A related species, the *Paeonia corallina,* commonly known as the male peony, is originally from the Caucasus and Syria. It is a little smaller and the flowers are not fragrant, and are simple (with only 5 to 10 petals), in coral-pink or bright red. This is not grown in the United States.

The florist's ranunculus is derived from *Ranunculus asiaticus,* a native of Eastern Europe and Western Asia or even China. It is a perennial, 5 to 15 inches tall, with large and fascicled roots, large and slightly indented basal leaves, and toothed upper leaves. The flowers are single, formed by 5 petals, or doubled, in whitish or yellow, red, lilac-pink, or violet. The stamens are numerous with gray-brown or almost purple anthers and surround the carpels. The seeds are in achenes.

The buttercups blossom in May and June and are used for edges, masses, rock gardens, and for cut flowers. They are propagated by root division. These are planted in fall and are dug after they bloom. It is possible to grow them from seeds, but they will bloom only after two years. They prefer loose soil and half shade with adequate moisture.

The cultivars with double flowers *(Ranunculus asiaticus flore pleno)* have an extraordinary resemblance to little roses.

81-83. Variety of *Paeonia albiflora* with double flowers.

84. Buttercup with double flower.

85. Buttercups of the cultivar *Ranunculus asiaticus flore pleno.*

88

Poppies

Even though sometimes a pest, the common field poppy *(papaver Rhoeas)* has a beautiful flower. Related species are decorative for their large, brightly colored or white flowers.

The most important species are *Papaver nudicaule, P. orientale* and *P. Rhoeas* (Papaveraceae family).

Papaver nudicaule or Iceland poppy is of artic-alpine origin, and is suitable for Alpine and rock gardens. It is biennial or perennial, 12 to 16 inches tall, and blooms from May through fall. It has thin, laciniate-toothed leaves. Its flowers are large; with white, orange or yellow petals numbering 4 or 5; and grow on long, thin stems. It is propagated by seed and needs well-drained soils and sunny locations. It grows best in cooler climates.

Papaver orientale or Oriental Poppy, is native to the Caucasus. It is perennial, grows from 1½ to 3 feet tall, is rough, erect, and has pinnate-toothed leaves. The flowers are large (up to 4 to 8 inches in diameter), normally red with a black throat, but cultivars with white, orange, or pink as well as with double flowers exist.

It is seeded in May or June in the seed bed using light soil; seedlings are thinned and later transplanted in August or September for flowering in the spring. Distance between plants should be from 15 to 24 inches. It is possible to propagate it by dividing the root clumps in the fall or by root cuttings inside the greenhouse during the winter.

Papaver bracteatum is a taller plant and the flowers, single or double and variously colored, may be 7 to 8 inches in diameter. The culture is similar to the oriental poppy.

The Opium poppy *(P. somniferum)* may not legally be grown in the U. S. and many other countries. It is native to Mediterranean Europe and Northern Africa.

The Shirley or Corn poppy *(P. Rhoeas)* is widely distributed over Europe and the Near East. Seed is sown early in the spring where it is to flower, and plants thinned to 6 to 8 inches apart. Flower color is red, pink, and white. It will commonly self-sow if seed is allowed to ripen.

86, 87. *Papaver nudicaule.*

88. *Papaver orientale.*

89, 90. *Papaver somniferum.*

91

92

93

Celosias or cockscombs

Within this group are the species of *Celosia* (Amarantaceae family). The most commonly grown are *Celosia Argentea* cv. *plumosa* (plumed cockscomb) and *C. Argentea* var. *cristata* (crested cockscomb), natives of tropical regions and introduced into Europe.

Plumed cockscomb produces conical and feather-shaped flowers. The crested cockscomb flower resembles a thick, crested and wavy fan. In both species, the colors range from yellow to fire-red, from pink-purple to a dark carmine and in some cultivars silver shades are seen.

These are annual, 15 to 24 inches tall (although dwarf cultivars may be only 8 to 12 inches), erect, little-branched, with alternate, wide, oval-lanceolate, dark green leaves. The flower cluster consists of numerous tiny flowers grouped together into a very compact mass. Seeds are small, kidney-shaped, black and shiny.

They are used for edges (dwarf cultivars), for mass plantings, and for cut flowers—especially to be dried for winter arrangements.

Seeds are sown in March or April indoors, the seedlings transplanted to small pots, and the young plants planted outdoors in May or June, 8 to 15 inches apart. They require full sun and bloom from May to September.

The *Celosia argentea* var. *cristata,* form *fasciata,* has peculiarly larger and curious clusters.

91, 92, 94. Cultivar of *Celosia argentea* cv. *plumosa.*

93. Group of *C. argentea* var. *cristata.*

95. A close view of the crested form, *C. argentea* var. *cristata* form *fasciata.*

96

Phlox

There are many species of phlox but two of the most interesting are *Phlox Drummondi* and *P. paniculata* (Polemoniaceae family), both native to North America. They grow from 1 to 3 feet tall with rigid stems. The basal leaves are oval-lanceolate and the upper leaves are large and rounded. The flowers are gathered in apical and axillary corymbs. Each flower is on a pedicel, and has a tubular corolla with a plain, round edge formed by 5 petals. Cultivars with double flowers have been developed. Flower color ranges from white to pink to purple, from yellow (rarer color) to red to violet and blue; they can be one color, shaded, spotted, or striped.

Phlox Drummondi is the original of the common annual phlox. It is seeded in February or March and planted outside in April or May. They bloom from May or June through September.

Phlox paniculata is a perennial, a little taller than the annual and blooms in August. It can be increased by division in late fall or early spring. It may be seeded during winter and planted outdoors when danger of frost is past. Among the perennial cultivars are: "Mia Ruys," with white flowers; "Fritiof," in lilac; "Frau Alfred von Mauthner," with red blossoms; "Riverton Jewel," with pink flowers; and "Amethyst" in dark violet.

96. Patch of *Phlox paniculata.*

98. *Phlox paniculata* var. *alba grandiflora.*

97, 99. Annual phlox, *P. Drummondi.*

100. Flowers of *P. paniculata.*

97

98

99

100

101

102

103

104

105

Columbines and bleeding hearts

The *Aquilegia vulgaris* or Columbine (Ranunculaceae family) is native to European and Asian mountain prairies, as well as, probably, to Algerian mountains.

It is a perennial, 1 to 3 feet tall, grows in clumps, and has thin, erect stems. The leaves have 2 to 3 leaflets with slightly or deeply toothed lobes. The flowers are formed by 5 sepals colored like the 5 petals, which elongate at the base into a spur. The color of the flowers varies from white to light pink, to lilac to blue, to blackish-violet. There are cultivars with double flowers, with the petals one inside the other, or with simple flowers, with very open almost nonexistent spur petals or those with very long spurs. The small and shiny black seeds are contained inside follicles in large numbers.

Aquilegia canadensis or American columbine has yellow and red pendulous flowers. Other species, with less flashy flowers, are cultivated for the beauty of their colors, often mixed with different shades. *Aquilegia caerulea* (Colorado Columbine) is bluish-white; *A. Skinneri* (Mexican Columbine) has yellow and red flowers; all have multi-colored hybrids.

Columbines bloom in early summer and are interesting in natural or rock gardens especially as isolated plants. They are seeded in early spring, transplanted to peat pots and planted outdoors either in spring or in fall. They prefer sandy soil and semi-shade. Distance between plants should be from 12 to 20 inches. It is important to remember that these plants are poisonous if eaten.

Bleeding hearts (*Dicentra spectabilis:* Ranunculaceae family) is very ornamental for its heart-shaped and swollen, white and pink flowers that are all in-line and pendulous from a long peduncle. It is perennial, a native of China and Japan, and blooms in May and June. It is used to make groups in semi-shade, particularly under trees and along slopes. It is seeded in fall; the plants spend winter under glass and are planted outdoors in spring at a 20- to 24-inch spacing. Propagation may also be by division in early spring.

101-104. Flowers of some cultivars of *Aquilegia vulgaris* (columbine).

105. *Dicentra spectabilis* (bleeding heart).

107

Foxglove, cleome, and acanthus

The foxglove (*Digitalis purpurea:* Scrophulariaceae family) is a native of Europe. It is a biennial plant, 2½ to 5 feet high, erect and rigid, not branched. The basal leaves are in a rosette and those on the stem are alternate; all are oval-lanceolate, rather wide, coarse, and velvety on the upper surface, and on the edges. The flowers are large, tubular in shape somewhat resembling a thimble as their corolla is of one piece. Color varies from lilac-carmine to pink to white, and internally is always white or lighter spotted. They are on a one-sided spike or raceme. The tiny, brown seeds are in bivalved capsules.

Foxglove blooms from June to August; it is used for patches of color in flower beds and is especially good in herbaceous borders. A robust plant, it does not present problems of soil or location. Seeds are sown in the spring or late summer and will bloom the following years. Spacing between plants should be from 15 to 24 inches.

There are several hybrids such as *Digitalis ambigua,* which has yellowish flowers and is very ornamental. The foxglove leaves are poisonous, and are the source of a common medicinal for people with heart disease.

The cleome (*Cleome spinosa,* Capparidaceae family), commonly called "Spider-Flower," is native to South America. It is an annual plant, grows from 3 to 4 feet high, and has one spiny erect main stem that is branched. Leaves are alternate, palmate-compound with 5 to 7 leaflets. Flowers are in large, erect apical racemes. Each flower has 4 oblong petals with long claws turned upward, and 6 long and thin stamens colored in purple with yellow anthers, giving a spidery appearance. The petals are pink-lilac or pinkish-white or white and sometimes with purple stamens. The seeds are small, yellowish, oblong-truncated, and irregular, in cylindrical capsules.

It blooms from mid-summer till fall and looks good in groups. Seed is sown in well-protected shelters in March or April, the seedlings transplanted into peat pots, and the young plants planted outdoors after frost. Distance between plants should be from 15 to 20 inches.

We include some species of the *Acanthus* genus (Acanthaceae family) of which the *Acanthus mollis* is the most common and the sturdiest. Another is *A. spinosus* with spiny leaves.

Acanthus is native to Europe, perennial, height 3 to 4 feet with large basal, oval, and lobate-toothed leaves in a thick rosette (spiny in *A. spinosus*). The large, irregular, labiate flowers are in large, thick spikes. Color varies from pinkish-white to lilac-rust, with some striping and a darker, hood-shaped upper edge.

It is used as an isolated plant or in groups. Propagation is by division in spring or early fall. It needs a well-drained, rich soil and full sun. It should be heavily mulched in the north since it is not reliably winter hardy there.

106, 108. *Digitalis purpurea.*

107. *Acanthus schottii.*

109. *Cleome spinosa.*

110

113

111

112

Scarlet Sages, delphiniums, and sweet peas

Three unrelated plants are included here, all having very ornamental flowers.

Scarlet sage *(Salvia splendens:* Labiatae family) is native to Brazil. It is cultivated as an annual, but it is perennial in the greenhouse. It grows from 15 to 30 inches tall although there are some dwarf types that reach only about 1 foot. It has opposite, oval and cordate, toothed leaves dark green above and grayish on the underside. The flowers are in apical spikes, each flower having a long, tubular, lipped, red corolla, with a large calyx of the same color. The seeds are small nutlets.

It blooms in July to September or until frost. It is excellent for edges (dwarf varieties), borders, and mass or bed planting. It is seeded in March or April under cover, the seedlings transplanted to peat pots, and the young plants planted outside when danger of frost is over, at a spacing of from 12 to 20 inches. It does best in sunny locations but may be grown in semi-shade. Cultivars with white, pink, red, violet or dark purple flowers have been developed.

Within the *Delphinium* genus (Ranunculaceae family), we distinguish two groups. The perennial delphinium is *Delphinium cultorum;* the annual is the larkspur, *Delphinium Ajacis.*

The larkspur is an annual herbaceous plant originating in Europe and the Orient, grows from 1 to 3 feet tall, has erect and rigid stems, with round leaves at the base of the plant and oblong above. The flowers are in apical spicate racemes; are not large; are irregular with the receptacle in the same color as the corolla, which is formed by 5 petals the highest of which is extended into a long spur. The seeds are small, round, and black, in follicles. The color varies from white to pink to blue to violet.

The larkspurs are suited for borders and for cut flowers. They are seeded indoors during spring, the seedlings transplanted to pots, and, the young plants planted outdoors after the last frost. They may also be directly seeded either in early spring or in fall. Distance between plants should be about 12 inches.

Delphinium are perennial plants derived from both European and Asiatic species. They grow to 25 to 40 inches or more, and have palmately-lobed leaves. The flowers are larger than larkspur and often wrinkled, and they form taller and bigger clusters. Flower color varies from blue to violet, to pink-lilac with white, pink, and light blue types. The "Pacific Giant" strain is among the best.

Delphiniums prefer sunny locations, cool summer temperature, and moist, well-drained, friable soils. They are seeded indoors in the early spring and then the young plants are transplanted outdoors. Seed sown in mid-summer produces plants ready for transplanting in September to flower the following spring.

The sweet pea *(Lathyrus odoratus:* Leguminosae family) is grown for its large, butterfly-shaped, fragrant, multicolored flowers, that bloom from June to September. It is annual and is normally seeded directly outdoors very early in the spring. It flowers best where summers are cool. A related species is the *Lathyrus latifolius,* the perennial sweet pea that has smaller flowers in white, pink, or carmine. It is sown in the spring and is transplanted in early summer.

110. *Salvia splendens,* scarlet sage.

111. *Delphinium cultorum,* delphinium.

112. *Delphinium Ajacis,* larkspur.

113. *Lathyrus latifolius,* the perennial sweet pea.

115

Anemones

Anemone coronaria, the Poppy-Flowered Anemone (Ranunculaceae family), is a common species grown in gardens and used as a cut flower by florists. It is a perennial, native to Central and Eastern Mediterranean countries. Erect and branched, it grows from 12 to 20 inches. Leaves are palmate, laciniate, and toothed; flowers have a cup shape and are formed by 5 to 10 petaloid sepals which are wide and round, in white or red, lilac, violet, purple, or blue, uniform color or variegated; the actual petals are missing. In the center of the flower is a thick crown of stamens with black or purple anthers that surround the carpels. The seeds are achenes.

Anemones bloom from April to June and are used for beds, borders, edgings, or for cutting. They may be seeded in the fall and carried over winter under protection, but they are usually propagated by planting rhizomes, remembering to plant the bud up. The division of the clumps is also possible. Spacing should be from 6 to 12 inches. These plants suffer from excessive cold and must be protected in northern areas. Double and semi-double flowered cultivars are available, the best strain being the "St. Brigid anemones"; among the cultivars with single flowers, the "de Caen" cultivar is excellent.

Other ornamental species are *Anemone japonica* (Japanese Anemone), a tall growing perennial with pink or white flowers and yellow anthers and *A. hortensis* (Garden Anemone) with lilac, pink or red flowers that are similar to *A. coronaria* of which there are several cultivars.

116

114-116. A few examples of *Anemone coronaria*

117. *A. coronaria,* a semi-double.

117

114

118

121

122

Fuchsias

Fuchsia (Onagraceae family) is grouped into the long-tube and the short-tube types, as well as into those having drooping flowers and those with erect flowers. They are native to tropical America. They are showy shrubs and their leaves are simple, oval-oblong, entire or slightly toothed, opposite or alternate or in whorls of three. The flowers are solitary or in groups in axillary or terminal clusters, mostly with long peduncles. The flower has a long, tubular calyx in red, lilac or purple, with four fleshy sepals usually curved backwards; the corolla is formed by four wide, rounded petals. There are double-flowered cultivars of great beauty, having a corolla of pink, lilac, purple, or white.

Among the less shrubby species, *Fuchsia megellanica* var. *globosa* grows about 1½ to 3 feet tall. It is used in borders, hanging baskets, or in pots and tubs.

Propagation is usually by cuttings in early spring under glass, which can then be transplanted into pots and protected over winter for planting outdoors the following spring.

Fuchsias need semi-shade, and sandy soil high in organic matter. Pruning is done during the fall. Fuchsias are generally injured by cold. They are carried over winter in a cool greenhouse.

Other species include: *Fuchsia fulgens* and its hybrids, with fall and spring bloom, and having flowers in many colors *F. splendens,* with summer blooming; and *F. speciosa,* with flowers in clusters. This latter species has been used in developing many of the present garden cultivars.

118. *Fuchsia megellanica* var. *globosa,* cultivar "Ridestar."

119. Cultivar "Melody."

120-122. Some examples of *F. speciosa.*

123

124

125

126

127

Zinnias

Most Zinnia varieties are cultivars of *Zinnia legans* Compositae family), a native of Mexico. 'hey are annual herbaceous plants 6 to 30 nches tall; they are erect, only slightly branched vith brittle stems; the leaves are rough like the tems, opposite, oval and light green.

Zinnia flower heads are of different sizes (from to 6 inches), are single or double, with a pro-ruding central disk, which has a crown of male lowers with yellow anthers around its edge. The ays are numerous ligules in various colors: vhite, greenish, yellow, orange, red, pink, lilac, urple. The seeds are elongated achenes over-opped by bristles.

Zinnias bloom abundantly from summer to all and are used for edges (dwarf varieties), bor-lers, massed plantings, and for cut flowers. They re seeded in April or May, the seedlings trans-lanted to peat pots, and the young plants lanted outdoors when danger of frost is past at 10- to 20-inch spacing. They may also be eeded directly outdoors. They prefer warm, unny locations and rich soil.

Cultivars with giant flowers (3½ to 6 inches in liameter) include "California Giant"; dwarf ypes with a large number of small, double flow-rs are the "lilliput zinnias" or "dwarf pompon innias."

Another species also suited for gardens is *Zinnia Haageana* or Mexicana zinnia.

123-127. Some types of *Zinnia elegans.*

128. Bed of *Z. Haageana.*

128

129

Carnations

Within the carnations, or clove pinks, we include the cultivars of *Dianthus Caryophyllu*
(Caryophyllaceae family).

The carnation is a perennial, 5 to 30 inche
tall, erect or drooping, branched with rigid, ligh
green, shiny stems having long internodes
Leaves are opposite, linear, and thick. The flowers are solitary or clustered, scented, with a
rigid, cylindrical receptacle having a double in
volucre and a corolla with many long deltoi
petals that have an indented or fringed margin
Flower color ranges from white to pink to yellow to red and maroon, and they may be of a
single color or shaded, spotted, or variegated
The seeds are small, oval, and contained inside
a capsule.

Carnations may be grown in gardens or in
flower boxes on terraces or porches, and a larg
greenhouse industry exists to sell cut flowers
They are seeded in early spring, the seedling
transplanted to pots when they have 5 to 1
leaves. The most common method of propagation is by cuttings, made in the greenhouse during winter. A heavy, fertile soil is preferred
Carnations will not tolerate cold or excessiv
heat. They are also susceptible to some diseases
such as alternaria and Fusarium wilt. Alternari
may be controlled by use of appropriate fungicides. Fusarium wilt-resistant cultivars shoul
be used outdoors. In the greenhouse, the soi
should be sterilized to avoid loss from Fusarium
Insects may usually be controlled by use of appropriate insecticides.

Many cultivars of carnations are available
some of which bloom almost continuously. Th
choice of flower color is practically unlimite
and plant breeders continue to develop hybrids
The hardy garden carnations, as the Enfant d
Nice or the Chabaud Giants, are better adapte
to garden conditions than the greenhous
florists' cultivars. These are seed propagated.

130 131

132 133

129-133. Examples of color in cultivars of *Dianthus Caryophyllus.*

Small-flowered dahlias

Small-flowered dahlias are the varieties of ahlias with flower heads 1 to 2 inches in diamter. They may be daisy-like with the central ellow disk surrounded by only one row of gules, or they may have globose and extra-douled flower heads formed by very many short, ollow, and conical ligules: these latter are nown as pompon dahlias. All these dahlias, as ell as those with large flowers illustrated on the ext page, belong to the hybrid series *Dahlia ortensis* (Compositae family) and derive from ome species such as the *Dahlia coccinea, D. innata, D. Merckii* and others, all native to lexico.

Dahlias are perennial, grow from 2 to 6 feet ıll, and have oblong-spindle-shaped, fleshy torage roots. Stems are erect and branched. eaves are opposite and may be simple, pinnate r bipinnate; leaflets are oval, toothed and darkreen. The flower heads are terminal on axillary eduncles, have a large involucre formed by two eries of green bracts and by a halo of rays; gules are wide or narrow, plain or twisted conical) in the various cultivars. The tubular entral disk, which is visible and yellow in the imple forms, is practically nonexistent in the oubled flowers formed largely of ray flowers.

Dahlias flower from July to October. They are xcellent in groups, borders (dwarf species with mall flowers), and for cut flowers. In early pring the storage roots are placed in a warm nd moist location. The roots generally are lanted outdoors directly after danger of frost is past, and as late as late June. They may be propagated by cuttings, taken in the spring from the young shoots sprouting from the storage roots. As soon as the cuttings have rooted, they are planted into pots until they have grown large enough to be planted outside. They are usually propagated by division of root clumps. These clumps are dug before frost and placed in a cool, dark, humid area, preferably in dry sand. There are many classes of dahlias based on the flower size and type ranging from the very large formal and informal decorative, cactus flowered, pompons, ball, collarette, and single types.

134

134. Group of "mignon dahlias" with simple flowers.

135. 136. Two "pompon dahlias."

137. Cultivar with slightly larger flowers.

137

139

138

140

141

142

Large-flowered dahlias

Dahlias with large flowers, reaching 10 inches in diameter belong to the same species mentioned on the previous page, *Dahlia hortensis,* with the same origins. The plants do not differ substantially from the small-flowered types except that they grow from 6 to 8 feet tall and have larger flowers. The flowers are of various types; sometimes with few (8 to 12) simple, flat ligules, sometimes with many ligules making semi-doubled flower heads (like peony flowers), and sometimes doubled or extra doubled.

The ligules may be of a single color or shaded darker towards the center of the flower. In other cases, the ligules are bicolored lengthwise (for example, white in the center and red at the edge) which is called "flamed."

A particularly interesting group of large flowered dahlias is the "cactus-dahlia," derived from *Dahlia Juarezii.* Their flowers are doubled and the ligules are long and twisted lengthwise, simulating long and rigid tubular petals.

The colors are variable in all large dahlias, having all the gradations of white, yellow, golden, orange, pink, red, carmine, lilac, dar purple, and violet; only blue is missing.

138. "Cactus-dahlia."

139. Example of dahlia with large, single flowers.

140. 141. Two large doubled dahlias.

142. A dahlia with "flamed" petals.

143

144

145

146

147

Chrysanthemums

On this page we describe the chrysanthemums other than the Korean types. Specifically here we are concerned with cultivars of *Chrysanthemum hortorum,* which might have derived from *C. indicum, C. sinense,* and perhaps from other species as well.

C. hortorum is perennial, somewhat shrubby, erect, 1 to 3 feet tall, and has rigid stems. The leaves are aromatic, oval or oblong, indented-lobous or pinnatifid, more or less toothed, green-gray above and lighter colored on the underside. The chrysanthemums of this group produce large flowers, solitary or in clusters, or in corymbs. The heads have numerous ray flowers, more or less narrow but mainly ribbon-shaped and curved towards the center of the head to form a beautiful globose mass. In many cultivars they are twisted or ruffled and then the whole flower head will look twisted and ruffled. The central disk can be seen but is always very small, greenish or yellow, or it may be absent.

They bloom from August through November. Planting stock may be purchased in the spring. They may be propagated by cuttings. Chrysanthemums need a light pruning in June or July to remove side branches so only 1 or 2 stems remain and to get large blossoms; it is important to remove the side buds on each stem leaving only the central bud. The pompon or hardy kinds have the tips of the shoots removed to induce branching and are not disbudded.

Chrysanthemums have numerous cultivars. Colors range from white to yellow to pink to carmine to golden brown to purple-rust.

Chrysanthemums are susceptible to aphids, which may be controlled with appropriate insecticides. Foliar nematodes may also be a problem, and may be controlled only by disinfecting the soil. Among the diseases, mildew and rust are possible problems, but may be controlled by using approved fungicides.

143. Example of Japanese chrysanthemum.

144-146. Standard chrysanthemums.

147. A spider chrysanthemum.

148

Garden chrysanthemums

Within this group we include the chrysanthemums having a more dwarf and bushy habit than those described on the previous page. The Korean types have smaller and thicker leaves and usually have many flower heads in large corymbs. They have been developed from *Chrysanthemum Koreanum* and *C. hortorum.* The flowers can be single, semi-double or double. The single flowers resemble daisies. The doubled types resemble the Japanese chrysanthemums, both in the shape and in the color, but are smaller. The cultivars with tiny button-like flowers are quite attractive.

These chrysanthemums are grown similarly to the larger flowered types. They are used in edges, beds, or in mass plantings, and may be grown in pots as porch or house plants.

---

148. Garden chrysanthemums mixed with Japanese chrysanthemums.

149, 150 Garden chrysanthemums, showing the large, central disk.

151. Garden chrysanthemum with daisy-like flowers.

152. Cultivar of chrysanthemum with tubular ray flowers.

upines

Both perennial and annual lupines belong to he genus *Lupinus* (Leguminosae family).

The prototype of the perennial lupines is considered to be *Lupinus polyphyllus,* a native of California. It is from 2½ to 5 feet tall and has rect stems. Leaves have long petioles, are palnately-compound, formed by 10 to 16 lanceoate leaflets, dull green on top and pubescent nderneath. The flowers, resembling a pea lower, are numerous and arranged on long, terninal racemes. Flowers are white, cream colred, pink, red, violet, or blue, of a single color r with the standard petal (the petal turned upvard) differently colored from those of the wings nd the keel.

The perennial lupines flower from June to September and are especially suited for massed groups. They are seeded in spring in pots or directly outdoors; the plants germinated in pots should be planted outside when they show the first leaves, taking care to avoid root damage.

A related species, *Lupinus Hartwegii,* of Mexican origin, has blue flowers with white or pink standard. It is generally grown as an annual.

Many species belong to the annual lupines: *Lupinus mutabilis* (also var. *Cruckshanksii*), *L. hirsutissimus, L. luteus,* and at least 10 others.

L. mutabilis is one of the most decorative and is from Peru. It grows from 30 to 50 inches tall, is smooth and shiny, and has branched stems shaped like a candelabra on the top of the plant. Flowers are scented and form thinner clusters than the perennials, but have the same color.

Seeds are rounded, yellowish and shiny, and grow in thick pods.

Lupinus hirsutissimus is a fuzzy and bluish lupine, grows to about 2 feet, and has scented, yellow flowers. The dwarf lupine (*Lupinus nanus*) grows to about 12 inches, has flowers with a white standard and blue wings, and is suitable for edging.

153-156. A few colors of some cultivars of *Lupinus polyphyllus.*

157

158

159

160

161

Sunflowers and rudbeckia (black-eyed-susans)

These plants belong to the same family (Compositae) and have in common a rugged appearance and yellow flowers.

The sunflower (*Helianthus annuus*) is a large annual, native to North America. It has a rigid and hairy stem with alternate, large and oval, dull and rough leaves, which are light green, toothed, and irregular. The flower heads are very large and may exceed 15 inches in diameter. They have a large, flat central disk that may be yellow, orange or brown, large ligules that can also be unicolored or bicolored in which case they present a darker basal crown around the disk. The seeds are large blackish achenes.

The sunflower blooms from July to September and is suitable for borders, for screening walls, and for groups. It may be seeded in late spring and transplanted outdoors after frost danger is past. Usually, it is seeded directly outside. Spacing depends on the cultivar. Single and doubled varieties exist, the latter with ligulated flowers even in the central disk. Some resemble gaillardias and have a brown disk, a red crown, and a yellow periphery.

The seeds are a source of an edible oil, and are used for feeding birds.

Related species include *Helianthus decapetalus* var. *multiflorus* and *Helianthus rigidus,* also native to North America and, like many other species (*H. atrorubens and H. tuberosus*), are perennial by creeping rootstocks. They grow as high as 10 feet and have large, underground rhizomes. Leaves and flowers are smaller than *H. annuus.* The dominant flower color is yellow.

The most rustic species is probably *Helianthus tuberosus,* known as Jerusalem Artichoke, which has large edible rhizomes. The perennial species can be reproduced by division of the rhizomes in fall or in spring.

Similar to the smaller sunflowers are the Rudbeckias, or Coneflowers (*Rudbeckia* genus), of which there are many species and cultivars suited to gardens. They are also native of North America. They have flowers with yellow ligules, with a protuding greenish disk (*Rudbeckia nitida*), or a brown-blackish one (*Rudbeckia subtomentosa*), or even with pink ligules and yellowish disk (*Rudbeckia purpurea* and *R. speciosa*).

They are perennial, bloom from July to October, and are used for borders or edges. Less sturdy then sunflowers, they require a light and well-drained soil. They are seeded either inside for transplanting, or directly outdoors. Distance between plants should be from 15 to 20 inches.

The Gloriosa Daisy has been developed from *R. hirta,* and is related to the Black-Eyed Susan. Flowers are single or double, golden yellow with a dark center, or with mahogany red at base. The plant grows from 2 to 3 feet tall and the flowers are 4 to 6 inches in diameter. Sown indoors and transplanted later, they will flower the first year.

157. Flower head of *Helianthus annuus* (sunflower).

158. *H. decapetalus* var. *multiflorus* (low-growing sunflower).

159. *H. tuberosus* (Jerusalem Artichoke).

160. *Rudbeckia hirta* (Black-Eyed-Susan).

161. *Rudbeckia subtomentosa* cv. "Goldsturm."

162

163

164

Hollyhocks

Plants of the botanical species *Althaea rosea* (Malvaceae family) are known as hollyhocks, and are sometimes called mallows. They are native to China.

Hollyhocks grow to a height of 6 to 9 feet, even though they are herbaceous. They are biennial or short-lived perennial and are erect and little branched. Leaves are alternate, on long petioles, large, rough, and light green. The flowers are large, axillary, almost sessile, developing along the stem. Each flower, in its simple form, has a large, funnel-shaped corolla, formed by 5 petals joined only at the base. The stamens are numerous and joined to form a column covering the ovary. The seeds are kidney-shaped.

Hollyhocks flower in the second year, from June to September. They are used for borders, beds, and for screens. They are normally seeded directly outside and thinned to stand 2 to 3 feet apart. Special types may be started inside, and should be allowed at least 6 inches per pot until planted outdoors. They can be propagated by division of the root clumps, or by cuttings using young growth. They are often infected with rust (*Puccinia malvacearum*), which may be controlled by use of appropriate fungicides.

The flowers are used by herbalists to make soothing medicants and the roots are used, like those of the Marsh Mallow (*Althea officinalis*), to prepare anticatarrhal teas and mucilage.

165

Cultivars with single, semi-double, and double flowers are available. The extremely doubled types resemble peonies. Dwarf cultivars, as well as tall, are rich in variously colored flowers: white, pink, lilac, red, crimson, reddish-yellow, or yellow.

162, 165, 166. Samples of double or extra-double hollyhock flowers.

163. Hollyhock with single pink flowers.

164. Semi-double flowers.

167

16

169

170

Plants with colored leaves and fruits

In addition to the flowering plants, color and interest can be enhanced by using plants having multi-colored leaves and brightly-colored fruit.

Among the foliage plants, the most popular is the coleus (*Coleus Blumei*) of the Labiatae family. It is perennial in the greenhouse but will not withstand frost. It grows from 1 to 2 feet tall, has an erect stem that is square in cross section and little branched. The opposite leaves are oval-pointed, toothed and sometimes laciniate, are yellow, green, or purplish and may be unicolored, striped, spotted, or margined. The flowers are labiate, not showy, and grow in terminal racemes. The seeds are small.

The *Coleus* are generally native to Malaysia and Australia. Because of their interestingly colored leaves, they are used for edgings, borders, mosaic patterns and hanging baskets. It is common to propagate coleus by cuttings in the greenhouse during winter, using stems taken from healthy plants. They are planted outside after danger of frost is past, 1 to 2 feet apart.

There are many named cultivars and several excellent strains grown from seed which are true to color and habit of growth.

Coleus are subject to damage from mealy-bug scale and from aphids, which may be controlled with suitable insecticides.

Species of the *Perilla* genus belong to the Labiatae family too, are native to China, and also have very ornamental colored foliage. *Perilla frutescens,* with its very pretty red-brown to blackish-purple leaves, is very well known.

Small plants, which produce brightly colored fruit that add so much beauty, include *Capsicum frutescens* and some *Solanum* (Solanaceae family). Within *Capsicum frutescens* is a dwarf pepper that develops very small, finger-shaped yellow or red fruits, and has dark green leaves. It is particularly good for borders, edging, and massed plantings.

Numerous species of the *Solanum* genus have colorful fruit, and most are perennial. They produce red, globose berries about 1 inch in diameter and are suited for flower beds and edgings. *S. Pseudo-Capsuum,* Jerusalem-Cherry, is used as a decorative pot plant for Christmas.

167. *Coleus Blumei,* cultivar with reddish leaves and yellow margin.

168. Example of a flower bed corner with yellow and purple *Coleus.*

169. *Capsicum frutescens,* small ornamental peppers.

170. A *Solanum* with red berries.

172

173

Clematis and morning glories

Clematis belong to the *Clematis* genus (Ranunculaceae family). They are perennial, are shrubby vines with thin, ropy stems, trifoliate leaves, and large flowers with 4 to 8, or more, petals. One of the most popular is *Clematis lanuginosa,* native of China, commonly known as large-flowering clematis. Its thin stem is knotty and multibranched; leaves are almost persistent, wooly and silvery when the plant is young, and becoming dark-green as the plant matures. Flowers are solitary or in groups of three, axillary, large (3 to 6 inches in diameter), formed by 4 to 8 petaloid sepals, variously colored from white to pink to lilac-blue. The stamens are numerous, whitish, and form a central tuft. The seeds are achenes with a persistent plumose style attached.

A related species is *Clematis patens* native to Japan, with blue flowers, while the hybrid *C. venosa,* has smaller (1½ to 2 inches in diameter) cream colored flowers. Numerous hybrids have been developed from crosses of *Clematis lanuginosa* and *C. patens,* sometimes called *C. hybrida* var. *grandiflora.*

Clematis are rugged plants with abundant bloom, and are suitable vines for covering walls, arbors, and treetrunks. They are propagated by cuttings or by grafting to maintain the flower characteristics. Grafts are made in spring or fall on *C. Flammula* or *C. Viticella* rootstocks. They prefer rich, well-drained soils and a light shade.

Morning glories are mostly annual (*Pharbitis, Ipomoea* and *Convolvulus* genera, often synonymous: Convolvulaceae family). *Convolvulus tricolor* is the common, three-colored morning glory. It is dwarf, growing only to 1 or 2 feet, has pubescent, little-branched, and drooping stems. Leaves are alternate, oblong-spatulate. The flowers are solitary, axillary, with long peduncles, funnel-shaped, large, with a corolla blue-violet at the edge and white inside with a yellow throat. Seeds are black, dull, angular, and contained in a capsule.

It is native to Southern Europe. It is used for hanging baskets and borders. It is usually seeded directly outdoors at about 12-inch spacings. It may also be propagated by cuttings. Cultivars are available with white, pink, or violet, either single-colored or bicolored, and either simple or double flowers.

The most popular of the Morning Glories is *Ipomoea purpurea,* native of the American Tropics, commonly known as Tall Morning Glory. It is climbing, annual, with heart-shaped leaves. The flowers are like *C. tricolor* but with a wider range of colors. It is seeded in late spring outdoors. Blossoming is continuous from July to September and often is spectacular. There are many related species.

171, 172. Two examples of *Clematis hybrida.*

173, 174. *Ipomoea purpurea* in two different colors.

175. *Convolvulus tricolor.*

176

Zonal geraniums

Commonly known as geraniums, these pelargoniums belong to the species *Pelargonium hortorum* (=*P. hybridum*= *P. zonale* X *inquinans*) and to the Geraniaceae family. They are plants native of Southern Africa. It is a perennial species in the greenhouse, but will not withstand freezing. It grows from 12 to 24 inches tall, sometimes higher. It has thick, cylindrical and branched stems with alternate leaves, which have a rather thick epidermis, are rounded and somewhat reniform, and have 5 to 12 lobes and a crenate edge. Leaves are light green or grayish with a concentric red or brown area and are velvety and scented. The flowers have 5 or more free petals and are in clusters of 5 to 30 or even more, in axillary umbels with long peduncles. The fruits are small, and contain 5 seeds.

They flower all year around if protected from freezing and are used in pots, as patio or house plants, in hanging baskets, and outdoors in beds and edges.

They may be propagated by seed sown during winter in pots, taking care to regulate the temperature and the moisture provided the seedlings. The most common method of propagation, however, is by cuttings taken in early fall and during the winter months and placed in pots with light, well-drained soil, in a cool greenhouse. They may be repotted in spring and placed in warm shelters to force the growth for outdoor planting.

Geraniums are subject to invasion by nematodes, which can be controlled by using sterilized soil. Green aphids sometimes infest geraniums.

The cultivated forms of *Pelargonium hybridum* are numerous and there are some with single and other with double flowers. Color varies from white to pink to bright red to dark carmine. Some are of a single color, some are bicolored. Some cultivars have variegated or white margined leaves (cultivar "Madame Salleron").

A related hybrid, *Pelargonium domesticum,* has scented, rounded-palmate leaves that are also toothed around the margins. In addition, it has large flowers (up to 2 inches diameter) in less numerous groups than the previous species. Many cultivars have flowers with a dark black-purple throat; the blooms are sometimes doubled and ruffled.

Pelargonium Radula, a rose-scented geranium, is a perennial, especially suited as a house plant.

176, 177, 180. Hybrids of *Pelargonium domesticum.*

178, 179. *Pelargonium hortorum.*

183

184

Ivy-leaved geraniums

The ivy-leaved geraniums, *Pelargonium peltatum* (Geraniaceae family) are from Southern Africa, with several natural variations.

Pelargonium peltatum is a perennial plant if protected from freezing. It is frequently grown in pots to decorate porches, verandas, terraces, walls, hanging baskets, etc. It has a green stem and branches that are rather woody, rigid and knotty, often hanging. Stems may grow 3 feet long and, are alternate, persistent, rounded but angular, thick, fleshy and hard, and bright green. The flowers, like the zonal geraniums, have 5 petals in globose umbels with long peduncles; simple and double forms are known. The color varies from white to all the gradations of cyclamen-pink to purple and to red.

Ivy geraniums prefer full sun and a soil high in organic matter. It is possible to take cuttings all year, although the best period is during late summer. They are kept indoors over winter.

185

181-183. Groups and plants of *Pelargonium peltatum.*

184. Cultivar with flowers having a purple throat.

185. Double-flowered cultivar.

186

187

189

188

Hyacinths

The following pages are devoted to some important bulbous or rhizomatous plants especially suited for gardens. One of the earliest of the flowering bulbs to bloom is the hyacinth, *Hyacinthus orientalis* (Lily family), a native of Syria and Mesopotamia. It has a bulb, is perennial, grows from 4 to 20 inches, with only basal leaves that are upright, linear, thick, shiny, and shorter than the inflorescence, which is a cylindrical-pyramidal raceme, thick, with a long scape. The numerous flowers are delicately scented, have 6 petals arranged in a star shape and curved backwards, with a corolla swollen at the base. The seeds are few, black, rounded, contained in three lobed capsules.

Hyacinths flower from February to April and are suitable for flower-boxes, pots, or forcing in bowls, as well as in the gardens in temperate climates where they are very suitable for edges and borders. The bulbs are planted in late fall, about 4 to 6 inches deep, in loamy soil, 4 to 6 inches apart. The bulbs may be removed after flowering, when the leaves are dry, and stored in a cool, dark place.

To force blooming during winter, the bulbs should be planted sometime between September and November in small pots with a light, rich soil, watered abundantly, plunging the pots into the soil in a cool place. When the plant sprouts, the pots should be taken into a warm shelter in full light such as in the greenhouse or in the house.

Propagation may be by seed, but plants will flower only after 4 to 6 years. Commonly, propagation is by planting the small bulblets that develop by the parent bulb.

Two main groups of hyacinths can be distinguished: Dutch Hyacinths with large inflorescences, and Miniature Hyacinths with fewer flowers on the spike. The flower colors vary from white to yellow, to pink to carmine-lilac and to violet-bluish with all the intermediate shades. Among the most popular cultivars are "Innocence" with white flowers; "City of Haarlem" (yellow); "Lady Derby" and "Queen of the Pinks," pink colored; the red carmine, "La Victoire"; and the sky-blue, "Grand-Maitre".

186. 188, 189 Variously colored hyacinths.

187. Close-up of an inflorescence.

Tulips

These plants offer the largest variety of shapes and flower colors among the flowering bulbs. They are primarily of two different species: *Tulipa Gesneriana* and *T. suaveolens* (Liliaceae family).

They are perennial, with oval bulbs having a reddish brown outer tunic. Leaves are oval, elongated, pointed, shiny and light green. The flowers, usually single and apical on a scape, are large, with 6 petals that form a cup. In the center of the flower is a short pistil with a large three-lobed stigma surrounded by 6 stamens with yellow, purple, or violet anthers. The seeds are dark and flattened, contained in a three lobed capsule.

Tulips bloom from April to June. The bulbs are planted in fall, 4 to 5 inches deep and 4 to 6 inches apart. They are removed from the ground after bloom when all the leaves have dried. They are propagated by the small bulbs around the parent bulb. Reproduction by seed is possible, but will not come true.

Tulips are subject to leaf and bulb rots caused by mildew *(Botrytis parasitica),* which can be controlled by fungicide treatment.

Cultivars of common tulips and the more valuable ones are usually *Tulipa Gesneriana,* including the Darwin Tulips that are of a single color, and the Rembrandt that are streaked or spotted. None of these are fragrant.

"Duc von Thol," earliest blooming and smallest flowered, with single flowers, unicolored or margined, are *Tulipa suaveolens.* These are mostly replaced by types merely called Early Single and Early Double.

The parrot tulips, having flowers with fringed petals, usually bicolored, are a form of *Tulipa Gesneriana* var. *dracontia,* or mutations of other types.

Other species also grown are: *Tulipa Kaufmanniana,* mainly with white petals inside and pink-violet outside; *T. Forsteriana* with elongated flowers; *T. praestans* which is multiflora; and *T. Clusiana, T. lutea,* and others.

It is customary to designate tulips developed by hybridization as *Tulipa hybrida* and to distinguish various cultivars, such as Triumph, Darwin, Cottage, Mendel, etc. Several thousand cultivars have been created by the skilled Dutch floriculturists. Among the best of the cultivars with simple flowers are: "Zwanenburg" (white); "Golden Harvest" and "Yellow Prince" (yellow); "Orange Wonder" and "Telescopium" (orange with thin streaks); "Princess Margaret Rose" (with yellow petals having flames of red on the sides); "Brilliant Star" (red-scarlet); "Cardinal" (red-carmine); "Clara Butt" (pink); "Aristocrat" (dark pink); "Demeter" (violet); "La Tulipe Noire" (a Darwin hybrid almost black); and "Pride of Zwanenburg" (bluish violet).

Double-flowered cultivars are: "Therose" (early yellow), "Orange Nassau," flame colored; and "Peach Blossom," peach colored.

Important parrot tulips are the cultivars: "Sunshine" (yellow); "Red Champion" (crimson); and "Violet Queen."

190

191

192

193

190. A tulip field.

191, 192. Cultivars of single-colored tulips.

193. A double-flowered tulip.

194

Narcissus-daffodils

Although both belong to the genus *Narcissus* (Amaryllidaceae family), it is customary to distinguish the narcissus as those having flowers shaped like stars formed by 6 petals and having a small cup or corona slightly ruffled on the margin in the center. On the other hand, daffodil is the common name for those that have a large conical or trumpet-shaped corona. Through hybridization it has been possible to obtain all intermediate shapes and sizes and even double types are now common, giving rise to the terms "small cupped," "medium cupped," "large trumpet," and "double."

Narcissus are perennial, originally from Europe; they have a pyriform bulb covered by a yellowish-brown tunic. The leaves are all basal, long and narrow, practically graminiform, but more fleshy, shiny green. The flower scapes are erect, one or more per plant, and have one or more flowers according to the cultivar. The flowers have 6 petals with a corona in the center.

Regardless of species or variety, narcissus are all suitable for borders, beds, and for potted plants. They bloom from March to May. They are cultivated and propagated as hyacinths, and should be spaced 8 to 10 inches apart. If propagated by seed, they bloom in four to six years.

The common Poet's Narcissus *(N. poeticus)* includes the "Poeticus" group, with fragrant, simple, white flowers having a yellow corona trimmed with red; both early and late cultivars are available. All are single flowered.

N. Jonquilla, commonly known as jonquils, have numerous (5 to 12), yellow flowers in an umbel. The paper-white narcissus, *N. Tazetta* v. *alba,* has white flowers with a corona and a medium sized cup that may be yellow or orange.

Hybrids of *N. poeticus* and *N. Tazetta* have resulted in the *Poetaz* group of narcissus, with larger flowers and a larger corona; the colors of the perianth vary from white to light yellow, with golden orange or almost red coronas. The "Scarlet Gem" cultivar is multiflowered, yellow with reddish corona; and the "Laurence Koster," is multiflowered and white.

Daffodils, *N. Pseudo-Narcissus,* are characterized by a well-developed corona with a tall crown and are white, yellow, or bicolored. These are hardy and can remain outdoors over winter.

Hybrids between the poet's narcissus and daffodils have produced the "incomparables" group, *N. incomparabilis.* They are uniflowered, with medium large and open corona, ruffled around the edges. "Scarlet Elegance" is a cultivar with a red corona.

The doubled types are derived from *N. Pseudo-Narcissus* and may have only a doubled corona or be completely double. They are typically completely of one color—yellow or white.

194. Group of daffodils.

195, 196. Hybrids of *Narcissus Pseudo-Narcissus;* Trumpet types.

197. A narcissus of the large-cupped type.

198

199

Various flowering bulbs

The Liliaceae, Amaryllidaceae, and Iridaceae families include bulbous and rhizomatous plants commonly used in gardens.

Three species of grape hyacinths are grown: *Muscari botryoides, M.racemosum,* and *M. comosum* (Lily family). They have a flower scape that rises from the tuft of linear or ribbon-shaped leaves, resembling hyacinths. Particularly interesting is *M. botryoides* which usually grows from 2 to 5 inches or a little more and has a mass of globose, pendulous, violet little flowers. The bulbs are planted in late fall and they will flower yearly; the small bulblets should be separated in early fall.

Crocuses belong to the *Crocus* genus (Iridaceae family) and are very low bulbous plants with a very early flowering—in February or March. *Crocus vernus,* also called early saffron, grows only 2 to 6 inches high and has narrow, linear leaves that are green with white veins. The white, violet, or yellow flowers have a chalice-shaped perianth of 6 petals. A related species, *C. aureus,* also called yellow saffron, is native to Eastern Europe and the Middle East; it has yellow flowers. The bulbs of the crocuses are planted during September to December, 3 to 4 inches deep and 2 to 8 inches apart.

The freesias *(Freesia refracta:* Iridaceae family) are bulbiferous, native to Southern Africa. They reach 8 to 15 inches in height, have narrow, parallel-veined leaves and the flowers have a tubular, funnel-shaped perianth in a spike inflorescence. The flowers are white, yellow, pinkish, orange, red, or violet. They are used for massed plantings, but may be cultivated outdoors only in regions with a mild climate. The bulbs are planted in October in light soil, and are dug and stored after they bloom. The variety *F. refracta* var. *grandiflora* is the most common. *F.refracta* var. *odorata* is brighter and darker.

Day lilies belong to the Lily family and are of the genus Hemerocallis. *Hemerocallis (cultivated: H. hybrida)* and *H. fulva* are hardy, grow 2 to 3 feet high or more. *H. flava* has yellow flowers and *H. fulva* red-orange flowers. Both species resemble lilies.

The Plantain Lilies, *Hosta ventricosa, H. Sieboldiana,* and *H. lancifolia* (Liliaceae) are shorter plants and the flowers grow in terminal clusters, first with a tubular, light violet perianth that opens into 6 petals. *H. plantaginea* has large, white, fragrant flowers that first look spindle-shaped and swollen; then, as they open up, they appear with 6 points at the apex. The leaves are oval-pointed wide and with curved veins more pronounced on the lower surface. Perennial, rhizomatous plants, they are used for edges, beds, and as specimen plants. They prefer cool climates and half shade. They are propagated by division in spring.

200

201

198. *Muscari botryoides* (grape-hyacinth).
199. *Sternbergia lutea.*
200. *Freesia refracta* (Freesia).
201. *Hemerocallis fulva* (day lily).

202

203

205

206

207

Iris

These plants, so well known for the shape and color of their flowers, belong to the genus *Iris* (Iridaceae family). Bearded irises of the *I. germanica* group and the bulbous irises of the *I. Xiphium* group are among the most interesting.

Both are perennial growing from 1 to 3 feet tall. The bearded iris has a cylindrical jointed rhizome that is often branched. The leaves are distichous, shaped like a sword-blade, shiny, and light green. The scapes are erect, rigid, and branched at the top to bear a group of flowers. Their perianth is 6 petals joined at the base.

The bearded irises include: the *Iris germanica* (with violet flowers), *I. germanica* var. *florentina* (with white flowers); and several others including those grouped as hybrids, *Iris hybrida,* which now include the majority of garden irises. They are characterized by large flowers whose 6 petals are similar three by three. The external three, the falls, are curved outwards and drooping and have short, yellow, soft and erect hairs along their middle line. The three interior petals alternate with the outer group, curve inwards, stand erect, and are called the standards.

Colors are various, ranging from white to a cream-color to yellow to pink-salmon to bright violet to dark blue to purple brown.

The bulbous group includes two species: *Iris Xiphium* and *Iris xiphioides;* the first is known as Spanish iris and the second one as English or Dutch iris. They are native to the Mediterranean regions. Their flowers have narrower and more rigid petals, which, with the stamens, acquire a three pointed appearance. *I. Xiphium* has narrower standards than *I. xiphioides;* the fundamental colors are yellow, white, and blue-purple and can be uniform or bicolored.

The rhizomes of irises are best planted in July or August or in early spring at a distance of 18 to 15 inches, and are left in place until they are crowded. They are propagated by division.

Bulbous irises are planted in the fall in mild climates, or in early spring in colder areas. These types are also suitable for greenhouse culture.

202. *Iris germanica,* or bearded iris, typical flowers.

203-205. *I. Hybrida,* bearded iris hybrids.

206. *I. Xiphium,* or Spanish iris.

207. A garden of bearded iris with several other perennials.

209

Gladiolus

Included here are the numerous species and varieties of the genus *Gladiolus* (Iridaceae family) that are cultivated in gardens. They are bulbous plants, native of Southern and Tropical Africa, the Mediterranean, and West Asia. The current garden types are all hybrid forms derived from these species and others, including *Gladiolus gandavensis, G. floribundus, G. psittacinus, G. Saundersii* and *G. purpureo-auratus.* They are perennial, from 2½ to 5 feet tall. The corm is globose, with a yellowish-red tunic. The sword-shaped leaves have a strong central vein and are light green. Flowers are large, in tall terminal spikes. Each flower has a rather irregular, almost bilabiate perianth of 6 oval, wide petals joined at the base and forming a deep throat. The seeds are brown, mostly winged, numerous, inside a three lobed capsule.

The size of gladioli and the beauty of their inflorescences make these plants suitable for cut flowers. In the garden, they are used in beds, borders, and rows. Colors range from white to the brightest shades of yellow, pink, orange, red, purple, and violet. Many cultivars have shaded, spotted, and streaked flowers.

Gladiolus corms are planted in early spring, 3 to 4 inches deep and 8 to 12 inches apart. After bloom, the flower stalks should be cut and after the leaves have dried, the corms should be dug and stored in a dry, cool place. They are subject to thrips *(Eliothrips hoemorrhoidalis)* which may be controlled by appropriate insecticides.

208-210. Cultivars of differently-colored gladioli.

211

Cannas and torch-lilies

Here, in conclusion are two rhizomatous plants with an erect habit suitable for groups or borders.

The floriferous canna is *Canna hortensis* or *C. hybrida* and derives from hybrids of *Canna indica, C. iridiflora, C. latifolia, C. glauca* and *C. annei* (Cannaceae family) all native of Central-Southern America. It is a perennial, 30 inches (dwarf cultivars) to 5 feet tall, with large rhizomes. The stems are erect and rigid, single and bear large, alternate, oval and pointed leaves that are light or dark green, sometimes reddish. The inflorescences are flashy, terminal, formed by two or more flowers that are protected by a green-leafy bract before they bloom. These flowers are irregular and large, with 3 green sepals, 3 yellow, orange or red petals (unicolored or spotted), and have 2 sterile, petaloid stamens. The large, round, and black seeds are in a nondehiscent capsule.

Cannas are propagated by division of the rhizomes, although the seed may be planted if desired. Rhizomes are planted each spring at a spacing of 1½ to 3 feet, and must be dug before frost each fall. They should be stored over winter in a cool, dry place.

The cannas are separated into two groups: those with flowers shaped like gladioli and those shaped more like orchids. The latter group are more generally grown.

Among the orchid-shaped canna flowers are: "Wyoming," orange flowers and red leaves; "City of Portland," pink; "Yellow King Humbert," yellow and red; "King Humbert," bright red. The dwarf Pfitzer cultivars are popular.

Torch lilies *(Kniphofia Uvaria-Tritoma uvaria:* Lily family) are rhizomatous and perennial, and grow from 3 to 6 feet tall. Leaves are all basal, long, ribbon-shaped and pointed, thinly ciliate around the edges. The stunning inflorescences are apical on racemes terminating the scapes, and have a conical shape with a thick tuft of numerous flowers of yellow, orange, or red, either unicolored or shaded. The seeds are black, angular, contained in three lobed capsules. They are native to Southern Africa.

They are seeded in pots in spring and transplanted outdoors after danger of frost is past. They are usually propagated by separating the rhizomes. They will not survive excessive cold or water and require a well-drained soil. They flower from July to September.

Cultivars vary in color from light yellow to reddish-orange. Related species are also cultivated among which *K. Caulescens* is a dwarf and has red flowers.

211. Canna flower.

212. *Kniphofia Uvaria,* cultivar "Canary."

213. A cultivar of torch-lily with red-orange flowers.